KICKING
the BUCKET
~ at the ~
# DROP
of a HAT

KICKING the BUCKET ~ at the ~ DROP of a HAT

The Meaning and Origins of Popular Expressions

Michael O'Mara Books Limited

First published in 2013 in hardback as *As Right as Rain*

This edition first published in Great Britain in 2016 by
Michael O'Mara Books Limited
9 Lion Yard
Tremadoc Road
London SW4 7NQ

A CIP catalogue record for this book is available from the British
Library.

Papers used by Michael O'Mara Books Limited are natural,
recyclable products made from wood grown in sustainable forests.
The manufacturing processes conform to the environmental
regulations of the country of origin.

ISBN: 978-1-78243-582-2 in paperback print format
ISBN: 978-1-78243-093-3 in ePub format
ISBN: 978-1-78243-094-0 in Mobipocket format

2 3 4 5 6 7 8 9 10

www.mombooks.com

Research by Elaine Koster
Illustrations by Andrew Pinder
Cover design by Patrick Knowles
Designed and typeset by K DESIGN, Winscombe, Somerset

Printed and bound by CPI Group (UK) Ltd, Croydon, CR0 4YY

Contents

To the **bitter** end
To **blaze** a trail
To **blow** a raspberry
To **blow** one's own trumpet
As **bold** as brass
A **bolt** from the blue
A **bone** of contention
To make no **bones** (about)
'**Break** a leg'
To **break** the bank
To **break** the ice
To give someone a **break**
A **bridge** too far
To **bring** home the bacon
To go for **broke**
Brownie points
To **burn** one's bridges
To **burn** the candle at both ends
To **bury** the hatchet
To **bust** a gut

Cack-handed
To **call** someone's bluff
A **cat** in hell's chance
To let the **cat** out of the bag
To be **caught** red-handed

Big **cheese**

Cheesed off

A (or an old) **chestnut**

To have a **chip** on one's shoulder

As **clean** as a whistle

A **clean** sweep

To take to the **cleaners**

The **coast** is clear

(A load of) **cobblers**

To get **cold** feet

To give someone the **cold** shoulder

Cold turkey

To **cost** an arm and a leg

Not all it's **cracked** up to be

Crocodile tears

To **cry** over spilled milk

To **cry** wolf

To **curry** favour

To **cut** the mustard

To **cut** to the chase

D   84

A **dark** horse

As **dead** as a doornail

A **dead** ringer

What the **dickens**?

To go to the **dogs**

Double whammy
Down in the dumps
Down to earth
Down to the wire
To **draw** a blank
Back to the **drawing** board
To **drive** someone nuts/to drive someone
    round the bend
At the **drop** of a hat
To **drum** up
To go **Dutch**

To **eat** one's hat
To **egg** someone on
To make **ends** meet

To **face** the music
Fagged out
Fair and square
A **far** cry (from)
In **fine** fettle
A **fish** out of water
As **fit** as a fiddle
A **flash** in the pan
Fly-by-night

With **flying** colours
To **foam** at the mouth
To put one's **foot** in it
Forty winks
To have a **frog** in one's throat
Full of beans

To give up the **ghost**
The **gift** of the gab
To **gird** up one's loins
To get someone's **goat**
To be in someone's **good** books
Goody Two-Shoes
It's (all) **Greek** to me
A **gut** feeling

Hammer and tongs
Hands down
As **happy** as Larry
To go **haywire**
Head over heels
Heads up
To bring to **heel**
Hell for leather
High and dry

No **holds** barred

(To eat) **humble** pie

To **kick** the bucket

A **last**-ditch effort

To **learn** the ropes

To **leave** in the lurch

To do one's **level** best

To go out on a **limb**

In the **limelight**

To be at **loggerheads**

Long in the tooth

By a **long** shot

Middle of the road

A **moot** point

To keep **mum**

Neck and neck

Neck of the woods

To get it in the **neck**

To **nip** something in the bud
The **nitty** gritty

Off one's own bat
Off the beaten track
Off the cuff

To **paint** the town red
Beyond the **pale**
To **palm** something/someone off
To **pan** out
Part and parcel (of)
Not a **patch** on
In a **pickle**
Pie in the sky
A **piece** of cake
From **pillar** to post
With a **pinch** of salt
To **pipe** down
In the **pipeline**
To go to **pot**
To **pull** out all the stops
To **pull** someone's leg
To **pull** the wool over someone's eyes

To **push** the boat out
To **pussyfoot** around

To take a **rain** check
Raining cats and dogs
To **rest** on one's laurels
To give one's **right** arm for something
As **right** as rain
To **ring** the changes
Between a **rock** and a hard place
To **rub** someone up the wrong way
Run of the mill

To get the **sack**
Up to **scratch**
To have a **screw** loose
All at **sea**
To **sell** someone down the river
To **shake** a stick at
Three **sheets** to the wind
On a **shoestring**
Short shrift
As **sick** as a parrot
By the **skin** of one's teeth
To **smell** a rat

Spick and span
A **stamping** ground
To **steal** someone's thunder
A **stick** in the mud
No **strings** attached
A **swansong**

To a **T**
To **talk** the hind legs off a donkey
On **tenterhooks**
That's the **ticket**
To **toe** the line
Every **Tom**, Dick and Harry
Tongue in cheek
A **turn** up for the books

Wet behind the ears
A **wet** blanket
To give someone/something a **wide** berth
The **world's** your oyster
The **wrong** end of the stick

Acknowledgements

Many thanks to Anna, Silvia, Jess and the rest of the team at Michael O'Mara Books; and to Elaine for dealing so competently with the fuzzy end of the lollipop.

Introduction

In case you're wondering, this is a book about idioms, so it seems only right to begin by clarifying what an idiom is. The *OED* describes it as 'a group of words established by usage as having a meaning *not deducible from the meanings of the individual words*' (my italics); other dictionaries emphasize the same point. An idiom, by definition, doesn't make sense.

Isn't that fun? Or is it just baffling?

Take the book's title, for instance. Why do we say 'as right as rain' rather than 'as right as snow' or 'as right as wind'? And why should rain, or any other climatic feature, be more right than anything else?

Why, to take another example, do we cry over spilled milk rather than spilled tea or spilled wine? Why is a wild idea pie in the sky or a piece of surprising news a turn up for the books?

A foreigner learning English might well ask these questions and be told, 'Because it just is, OK?' That's because a newcomer to the language has to learn the exact form of an idiom – nine times out of ten, if you translate it from one language to another, it means nothing, and if you alter a single word it means even less. (To give someone the cold elbow? To bring home the pork? I don't think so.) But if you want to delve deeper, to find out where these apparently absurd expressions came from in the first place, you might choose to pick up this book. It's an attempt to reduce the bafflement and increase the fun.

When I wrote a book of proverbs, *An Apple a Day*, a few years ago, I found that, like a lot of the English language, many of them derived from the Bible or the works of Shakespeare. The idioms in *Kicking the Bucket at the Drop of a Hat* tend to have humbler beginnings. They often come from worlds that have their own specialist vocabulary, such as seafaring (see TO THE BITTER END and TO PIPE DOWN), horse-racing (NECK AND NECK and HANDS DOWN), baseball (TO TAKE A RAIN CHECK) or politics (MIDDLE OF THE ROAD). Expressions coined in these settings, often with a practical purpose, are then taken up by journalists and other writers and used out of context. At first they may be enclosed in semi-apologetic inverted commas or, in Britain, accompanied by the proviso 'as the Americans say'. But these asides soon disappear as the phrase becomes accepted. Thus it moves from the specific to the general, from the literal to the metaphorical, from the inventive and original to the everyday – but with one thing in common. It sticks resolutely to the same form of words, even though that form of words no longer makes sense. It becomes an idiom.

That isn't to say that the Bible and Shakespeare have no place here. We owe the former TO GIVE UP THE GHOST and TO GIRD UP ONE'S LOINS, and the latter THE BE-ALL AND END-ALL and IN A PICKLE. This raises another point about idioms: having become fixed in the language, they may keep alive a word, or a specific meaning of a word, that is otherwise lost. The 'ghost' in TO GIVE UP THE GHOST means the human spirit, the aspect of a being that leaves the body after death; that sense is hardly ever used in modern English, except in this expression. SPICK AND SPAN is an example of two words that have become obsolete ('span' in this context means a chip of wood, nothing to do with the current senses of the length of a bridge or the duration of a life). Yet they persist in this one idiom.

Digging down into the history of language is not an exact science. The first recorded use of an expression often shows that it is well established – the writer clearly expects his readers to know what he means – so it's impossible to be precise about when it was invented. On rare occasions (see, for example, BACK TO THE DRAWING BOARD and TO STEAL SOMEONE'S THUNDER) we can be more or less certain; sometimes, we have to admit that we simply don't know. In between, it is not uncommon to come across an explanation that sounds plausible and has gained wide acceptance but has later been found to be highly unlikely (see BEYOND THE PALE).

So what can we do? Only our humble best. Aim at the truth, admit it when we don't know and tell a few good stories along the way. There is no shortage of those. As Dr Johnson didn't say but should have, if you are tired of the English language you are tired of life.

Caroline Taggart

A

Above board

'Board' in this context is another word for 'table' and if you keep your hands above it people can see what you are doing. Specifically, if you have cards in your hand when playing poker or the like, they can tell that you are not – accidentally, of course, because you happen to be wearing that sort of jacket, not because of any intent to defraud, how could you think of such a thing – pulling *an ace from your sleeve* (see next entry). The phrase – meaning honest, open, FAIR AND SQUARE – dates back to the sixteenth century in its literal sense and has been used in a figurative sense almost from the word go.

Oddly, if we want to convey skulduggery, we say *underhand* rather than *under board*. And, to complicate the issue, I discovered in the course of my research that there exists a company called Interface that produces a range of 'tufted cut and loop' wood-effect carpet tiles called Above Board. So you could, should the mood take you, have something above board underfoot.

To have an ace up one's sleeve

This means to have a good thing hidden away, to be kept secret until you need to use it. Like ABOVE BOARD, it derives from card playing, where in many games an ace is a high card, a potential winner. Early (nineteenth-century) uses in both the UK and the USA refer to games of chance; then in 1916 the *OED* records this extended metaphor: 'You tell a man your cards are all on the table and try to take him into your confidence, but unless he has confidence in you he suspects that there are

some aces up your sleeve.' This could, of course, be interpreted literally, except that it comes from the *Electric Railway Journal*. The May 1916 edition of that worthy publication includes articles on 'Detroit Tunnel River Operation', 'Latest Connecticut City Cars' and 'Franchise Extension Rejected in Valparaiso, Chile' – so it's unlikely to have slipped in anything about cheating at cards; the author is talking about one railway company doing business with another and we can safely say that this is the earliest truly idiomatic use.

The Americans also use an equivalent expression, *to have an ace in the hole*. This is said to originate specifically from poker, where a 'hole card' is one that is dealt face down and is therefore hidden from one's opponents. The implication is that an ace would be the best possible card to have hidden away, though anyone who has played poker will know that it is not as simple as that.

Against the grain

The grain here is 'the general direction or arrangement of the fibrous elements in wood', which makes cutting *against the grain* – i.e. crosswise – more difficult than cutting in line with it; it will also result

21

in a torn, jagged edge rather than a smooth one. Thus something that goes metaphorically *against the grain* is difficult, unnatural and unpleasing. The expression is, however, often followed by *but*, with the speaker making an unwilling concession: 'It goes against the grain to agree with your father, but in this instance I think he has a point.'

The first recorded use is in Shakespeare's *Coriolanus* (*c*.1605), when the tribunes are trying to persuade the people to change their minds about appointing the arrogant Coriolanus to the high post of consul:

> *Say, you chose him*
> *More after our commandment than as guided*
> *By your own true affections, and that your minds,*
> *Preoccupied with what you rather must do*
> *Than what you should, made you against the grain*
> *To voice him consul: lay the fault on us.*

It's a bit complicated, and this is perhaps not the place to go into the minutiae of politics in Ancient Rome, but it boils down to: 'Admit you've made a mistake and blame us.' More manageable is this quotation from Winston Churchill:

Certainly the prolonged education indispensable to the progress of Society is not natural to mankind. It cuts against the grain. A boy would like to follow his father in pursuit of food or prey … He would like to be earning wages however small to help to keep up the home. He would like to have some leisure of his own to use or misuse as he pleased.

If you remember that Churchill, by his own admission, did badly at school, or at least badly in the subjects that didn't interest him, you'll see that these words came from the heart.

All and sundry

Nowadays this is a rather dismissive term for 'everyone', suggesting that 'everyone' includes the riff-raff or the relatives you felt obliged to invite but are really hoping won't come. It dates back to the fourteenth century and its origins are legal: 'all' and 'sundry' basically mean the same thing, and saying the same thing twice is one of the many ways in which legalese tries to avoid loopholes and ambiguity. Or, as William Safire put it in his *Political Dictionary* (2008): 'Legalese often has the virtue of eliminating ambiguity, and should be read more as a mathematical equation than as prose, anything herein to the contrary notwithstanding.'

To have an axe to grind

Meaning 'to have a private reason for doing something, to have an ulterior motive', this comes from a story attributed to the American politician and polymath Benjamin Franklin (1706–90). It tells the cautionary tale of a man who asks the local blacksmith to sharpen his axe particularly thoroughly and is tricked into doing the heavy work of turning the grindstone himself. Although Franklin doesn't use the form of words, the story was sufficiently well known for a later politician, Charles Miner (1780–1865), to write, with a clear nod to his predecessor, 'When I see a merchant over-polite to his customers ... thinks I, that man has an axe to grind.'

By the time the expression had crossed the Atlantic it had taken on the added meaning of having a score to pay off, of being tinged (to put it no higher) with resentment. James Joyce used it in *Ulysses* (1922):

> *Skin-the-Goat, assuming he was he, evidently with an*
> *axe to grind, was airing his grievances in a forcible-*
> *feeble philippic anent the natural resources of Ireland*
> *or something of that sort …*

Which – at least by Joyce's standards – makes the new meaning perfectly clear.

B

As bald as a coot

This expression, meaning 'completely bald', has been around since the fifteenth century, but is both unkind and inaccurate. Unkind because it tends to be used disparagingly – as if being bald is more or less OK, but being *as bald as a coot* is somehow ridiculous; and inaccurate, because coots are *not* completely bald. They have a white, featherless frontal plate on what ornithologists probably don't call their forehead; this gives an impression of *receding* hair. But from the crown of the head all down the back to the tail they are black and aren't any more bald than most other healthy birds.

If you wanted to be accurate and stick to the avian theme, *bald as a vulturine guineafowl* or *bald as a lappet-faced vulture* would serve your purpose – these birds are genuinely bald-headed for reasons to do with their feeding habits, which are too distasteful to go into here. If you feel these don't quite trip off the tongue, you could try sticking to *bald*. Or just don't mention the subject at all.

On the ball

The consensus is that this derives from *keeping your eye on the ball* in a sporting context, meaning staying alert, focusing on the important aspects of what's going on. As a metaphor, it is comparatively recent: the *OED*'s earliest citation dates from 1939 and is American; in 1961 the British literary magazine *The Listener* was still putting it in inverted commas and adding 'as the Americans would say' – though that, of course, may just have been *The Listener* being precious. By the time of the 2002 football World Cup the expression was sufficiently established for Ant and Dec to record an anthem with the title 'We're on the Ball'. This peaked at Number 3 in the pop charts and one shudders to imagine what *The Listener* would have made of that.

To bark up the wrong tree

This is something that misguided dogs do when they are hunting raccoons.

No, honestly, it is. It comes from American hunting parlance of the nineteenth century. Raccoons are nocturnal, so it made sense to hunt them at night when they were up and about. The idea was that a dog would flush out a 'coon, which would take refuge in a tree; the dog would then stand under the tree and bark until his master arrived with a gun and shot the quarry, to turn its skin into one of those fur hats with a tail that pioneers such as Dan'l Boone and Davy Crockett used to wear.

However, raccoons are crafty creatures and perfectly capable of scrambling from one tree to another, so a dog that didn't have all his wits about him might be left … You've guessed it.

The expression didn't stick to dogs for long: by 1832 it had extended its meaning to encompass a person who had got hold of THE WRONG END OF THE STICK.

Bats in the belfry

Nowadays we tend to think of belfries as bell towers, because of their opening syllable, but in fact they didn't originally have anything to do with bells. Way back in Norman times a belfry was simply a watchtower – the confusion came when the Norman French word was adopted into English, where the unrelated 'bell' already existed.

No matter. The point is that a belfry is a tower and, because of its distance from the ground, came to be used – in the USA in the early twentieth century – as a slang synonym for head. At around the same time the word 'batty', which Shakespeare had used to mean literally 'resembling a bat', was given the modern sense of eccentric or even crazy. The inspiration is presumably the way that bats in a confined space seem to fly around hectically and randomly; thus if someone is batty their thoughts and ideas are all over the place. It is a small step from describing someone as 'batty' or 'bats' to assigning the bats to the afflicted person's metaphorical belfry.

The concept isn't new: in Regency times someone who 'wasn't quite all there' could be described as *queer in his attic* or *touched in his upper works*, and a generation later Charles Dickens used *rats in the garret*, but the pleasing alliteration of 'bats' and 'belfry' doubtless explains why this expression has won out over time.

The be-all and end-all

This turn of phrase first appears in Shakespeare's *Macbeth* (1606), when Macbeth is trying to talk himself into murdering Duncan. He wishes that the killing blow might be the *be-all and end-all* – in other words, that the deed would be enough to make him king without his having to do anything else about it. Funny to think that he can contemplate slaughtering a man who is his king, his kinsman and his guest, yet baulk at indulging in political shenanigans afterwards, but who are we to take issue with the Bard?

Over the years this meaning has changed, so that since the nineteenth century *the be-all and end-all* has been not a deed but a concept, either something that is complete or supreme of its kind – the last word, if you like – or an ultimate aim. The IMDb plot summary of the 2009 movie *The Be All and End All* tells us that 'at fifteen, Robbie has only one thing on his mind – losing his virginity.' I think that gives us the gist.

To beat about/around the bush

Beating about the bush or, if you want to be picky about it, the bushes or undergrowth, is what beaters do during a shooting party, in order to flush out the game so that the 'guns' can shoot it. Because you can't be sure exactly where the game is hidden, it is by definition a rather imprecise activity, whereas the actual shooting, if you are any good at it, is accurate and timed to a nicety. The expression was used in a literal sense as early as the fifteenth century; it had evolved into the metaphor of 'approaching in a roundabout way, prevaricating and avoiding getting to the point' by the end of the eighteenth.

To beaver away

Beavers are busy creatures: they work hard chewing through tree trunks, damming rivers and building themselves lodges. They are mostly found in North America, so it is not surprising that this expression – meaning simply to work hard and persistently – should have originated there. It's of comparatively recent date, the first recorded use being in 1946.

Beavers were once also found in the UK – the Yorkshire place name Beverley means 'beaver lodge' and there is still a beaver on the town's coat of arms. There aren't any beavers wild in the area, though: for that you have to go north, to Argyll in Scotland, where, in the UK's first formal mammal reintroduction scheme, they have recently been reintroduced. In this instance it is the conservationists, rather than the animals themselves, who have been *beavering away*.

A bed of roses

In Christopher Marlowe's poem 'The Passionate Shepherd to His Love' (published posthumously in 1599), the shepherd makes all sorts of wild promises, including:

And I will make thee beds of roses
And a thousand fragrant posies.

This is one of the first recorded uses of the expression, and we are left to assume that the young lover meant rose petals, or that he was at least planning to remove the thorns. This impractical-but-literal sense has developed into a figurative one, whereby a bed of roses can be any comfortable, easy-to-deal-with situation. Very often nowadays we are told that a particular set-up or life in general is *not* a bed of roses. As if we didn't know that.

To make a beeline for

To head directly towards, as bees were once believed to do when returning to the hive. This expression is first found in the USA in the early nineteenth century – about the same time as the Swiss naturalist François Huber's hugely influential *New Observations on Bees* was translated into English. Huber wrote some extraordinarily personal observations on the mating habits of the queen honeybee, so perhaps, in the days before internet porn, apiarists everywhere were beginning to study their little friends more closely.

By the time Edgar Allen Poe wrote *The Gold Bug* in 1845, the expression was well established. His characters, attempting to decipher an encoded message they have found on a piece of parchment, come up with:

A good glass in the Bishop's hostel in the Devil's seat – forty-one degrees and thirteen minutes – northeast and by north – main branch seventh limb east side – shoot from the left eye of the death's-head – a bee-line from the tree through the shot fifty feet out.

If I tell you that the Bishop's hostel turns out to be a rock formation, the Devil's seat a niche in a cliff and the death's head a human skull that can be seen only through a 'good glass' or telescope, you'll see that working out what 'a bee-line' meant was the least of anyone's worries.

To bend over backwards

To make a very great effort, normally to be helpful/ fair/unbiased – *bending over backwards* being one of the most uncomfortable things you can ask your body to do. If you don't believe me, check out the poster for the film *The Last Exorcism Part II*, in which Ashley Bell, playing the girl in need of a second 'last exorcism', bends over backwards far enough to form a graphic figure 2. It looks very painful indeed, but that may be because Ashley is also supposed to be giving the impression that she is possessed by the Devil.

One of the earliest citations for the expression comes from a 1927 edition of the American political periodical *The Nation*; it tells us that 'Stambuliski leaned over backwards in his desire to satisfy Serbian demands.' Aleksander Stambuliski (sometimes written as Stamboliyski, but it's the same guy) was prime minister of Bulgaria in the aftermath of the First World War and you can imagine that trying to sort out the various Balkan Questions at that time would have required more than bodily contortions.

To go berserk

To run amok, go bananas, go ballistic or in some other way lose control of yourself through rage or insanity. The Berserker, the *OED* tells us, was 'a wild Norse warrior of great strength and ferocious courage, who fought on the battle-field with a frenzied fury known as the "berserker rage"'. No one is really sure where the word came from, though it may derive from 'bare sark', meaning that this wild warrior – a hardy Northern soul – fought in his 'bare shirt'. Or, less hardily, in a bearskin shirt.

Nineteenth-century writers frequently referred to 'a Berserker rage' or likened wild behaviour to that of the Berserkers; it was English novelist Henry Kingsley (brother of Charles of *Westward Ho!* fame) who first made the leap towards the modern metaphor. In *Silcote of Silcotes* (1867), he wrote, 'With her kindly, uncontrollable vivacity, in the brisk winter air she became more "berserk" as she went on.' But it was not until 1940 (and in the USA) that the expression really caught on: the *Chicago Tribune* of 20 November of that year kindly explained that the word 'berserk' had recently been added 'to the slang of the young and untutored' as a synonym for 'crackpot behaviour'.

To take the biscuit

Or *cake*, if you prefer. Either way, it means to be the most outstanding or possibly the most outrageous or ridiculous example of its kind. *To take the cake* seems to have originated in the southern United States in the nineteenth century, when a form of entertainment in the black communities was for couples to promenade arm in arm. The prize for the most stylish couple was often a cake; the competition thus became known as a 'cake-walk' and the prize-winners were said to *take the cake*.

The expression had appeared in British English by the 1880s, but then was frequently replaced by *to take the biscuit* (goodness knows why – it's not as if we didn't know what cakes were) and in the hands of sardonic writers such as George Bernard Shaw acquired its pejorative sense. In *John Bull's Other Island* (1904) he has one character say to another (and I'm translating from Shaw's idiosyncratic spelling here): 'All you know is how to howl about it. You take the biscuit at that, you do.'

In 1999 a British scientist won an Ig Nobel Prize for his work into dunking biscuits. The BBC News website reported that 'the Bristol researcher ... wrote an equation to show what happens when the starch globules in a biscuit absorb liquid, producing a gunge that breaks off and falls to the bottom of the cup. From this, he was able to advise everyone on the technique that would result in the perfect dunk.' Inevitably, the report bore the headline 'Brits take the biscuit'.

To the bitter end

Well, it means 'to the end', obviously, but to the end no matter what, regardless of the consequences or the sacrifices that need to be made. Its derivation is more fun than it might at first appear, because it is likely to have been influenced by two of the most prolific sources of idioms: seafaring and the Bible.

Aboard a ship, the posts, set firmly into the deck, round which cables are coiled, are called the bitts, so to unravel something *to the bitt* or *bitts' end* is to unravel it to the very end, leaving no margin for error. Completely unconnected to this, in the biblical book of Proverbs, there is this stark warning against adultery:

For the lips of a strange woman drop as a honeycomb, and her mouth is smoother than oil: but her end is bitter as wormwood, sharp as a two-edged sword. Her feet go down to death; her steps take hold on hell.

It is likely that *to the bitter end* originated in the nautical context, was influenced by the biblical one and, by the middle of the nineteenth century, ended up being the way it is because most of us are more familiar with 'bitter' than we are with 'bitts'.

New York's oldest rock club is called The Bitter End: its website lists many, many international names who have played there, from Woody Allen to Neil Young. I mention it only because that long list includes THE NITTY GRITTY Dirt Band.

To blaze a trail

It might be tempting to think that 'blazing' a trail had something to do with setting fire to the undergrowth in order to create a path through unexplored territory. It sounds a suitably pioneering thing to do, as the idiom means just that – to pioneer, to set a course for others to follow.

But no. The blazing here is connected not with fire but with notches being cut into trees to leave a series of white marks (similar to the blaze on a horse's nose) clearly visible to anyone coming along behind you. In its literal sense the expression does indeed date back to pioneering days in North America; its figurative use is first found in the early twentieth century and the noun and adjective 'trail-blazing' some fifty or sixty years later.

To blow a raspberry

Cockney rhyming slang. 'Raspberry' is short for 'raspberry tart'. Need I say more?

Well, yes, OK. The *OED*'s earliest citation comes from an 1890 *Dictionary of Slang* and explains the concept thus: 'The tongue is inserted in the left cheek and forced through the lips, producing a peculiarly squashy noise that is extremely irritating. It is termed, I believe, a *raspberry*, and ... is regarded rather as an expression of contempt than of admiration.'

Nine years later, Arthur M. Binstead's *Gal's Gossip* has: 'a loud and offensive noise, like the rending of glazed calico, made by obtruding the wet tongue between the closed lips, and by low cabmen and persons of that class, called a "raspberry", came from the gallery.'

The category 'low cabmen and persons of that class' was later tacitly extended to embrace the great comedic writer Spike Milligan: in 1976 he co-wrote (with Ronnie Barker) a serial entitled 'The Phantom Raspberry Blower of Old London Town' for the *Two Ronnies* television series. The plot centred on a Jack the Ripper-style murderer who dispatched his victims by blowing a raspberry at them. The credits at the end of each episode included the rarely seen 'Raspberries professionally blown by Spike Milligan'.

To blow one's own trumpet

To boast about one's own achievements, loudly and brassily. The concept of a trumpet being used to celebrate a triumph is an old one, dating back to the King James Bible (1611) and beyond; the idea of doing it for yourself is found in the mid-nineteenth century and crops up, clearly as a familiar idiom by this time, in Gilbert and Sullivan's *Ruddigore* (1887):

> *If you wish in the world to advance,*
> *Your merits you're bound to enhance,*
> *You must stir it and stump it,*
> *And blow your own trumpet,*
> *Or, trust me, you haven't a chance!*

The worst thing with which a man can be 'saddled or hampered or addled', the song maintains, is 'a diffident nature'. But this is Gilbert, remember. He was a satirist. Don't take him at his word. You may find yourself losing friends.

As bold as brass

Legend links this expression – which means unshamefacedly bold, not caring what anyone thinks – to a Mr Brass Crosby, Lord Mayor of London in 1770. Various printers had published accounts of parliamentary debates, which was at the time considered a breach of parliamentary

41

privilege. Crosby loudly and tenaciously stood up for freedom of speech, refusing to prosecute the printers concerned and saying that it was in the interest of the citizens whose rights he was sworn to protect that such matters be made public. He went to jail (in the Tower of London, no less) as a result, but became very popular with – well, lots of people who weren't MPs. It is as a direct result of this incident that *Hansard*, the verbatim account of Parliament's proceedings, came into being. So Brass Crosby is one of those all-too-common historical figures: a great and important man of whom most of us have never heard.

Did he have anything to do with *as bold as brass*? It's difficult to be sure. The association between the shiny, hard and rather flashy metal and barefaced cheek dates back a lot further: 'brazen' in this sense is found in 1573 and 'brassy' in 1596. But *as bold as brass* came along a lot later: it appeared in print for the first time not twenty years after Mr Crosby's contretemps, in George Parker's *Life's Painter of Variegated Characters in Public and Private Life*: 'He died damn'd hard and as bold as brass. An expression commonly used among the vulgar after returning from an execution.' It may well be that 'the vulgar' had latched on to Mr Crosby's first name and attached it to a common metaphor. As with BATS IN THE BELFRY, the alliteration would have helped the expression catch on.

A bolt from the blue

An extremely unlikely event, such as a thunderbolt appearing from a blue sky. The concept isn't new – it is found in one of Horace's *Odes* from the first century BC – but the first recorded instance in English comes from Thomas Carlyle's history of the French Revolution, published in 1837. He remarks that 'Arrestment, sudden really as a bolt out of the Blue, has hit strange victims.'

Having said that, it doesn't do to be too cocky about bolts from the blue. The US Government National Weather site – on its page on Lightning Safety – tells us that a bolt from the blue is 'a cloud-to-ground lighting flash that typically comes out of the back side of the thunderstorm cloud; travels a relatively large distance in clear air away from the storm cloud and then angles down and strikes the ground'. And, of course, strikes you if you happen to be hanging about.

'Lightning,' the site continues, 'can and does strike many miles away from the thunderstorm cloud itself.'

You've been warned. Stay indoors.

43

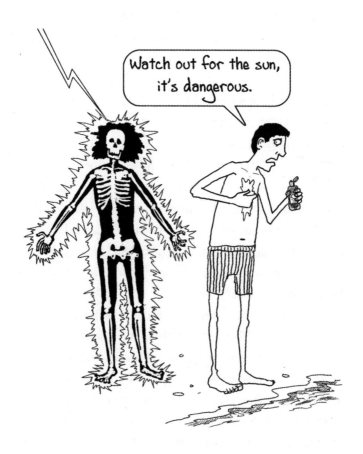

A bone of contention

If you're a dog, or perhaps if you are two dogs, any bone is likely to be *a bone of contention*. All it means is that you are going to fight over it. Or, once you have turned back into a human, you are going to argue about the matter under discussion. The idea goes back to the sixteenth century, when just 'casting a bone' between two people was enough to cause strife; *bone of dissension* is found in 1596 and the current wording in 1711.

To make no bones (about)

The ancestor of this expression, which dates back to the sixteenth century, is *to find bones in*, meaning to make objections or difficulties about doing something. The traditional explanation is that if you find bones in your soup (particularly if you are a vegetarian), you feel you have a right to complain. This evolved into *to make bones,* to make a fuss, particularly to make more of a fuss than the situation warranted. Thus *to make no bones was not* to make a fuss but to get on with doing whatever was required.

Nowadays *to make no bones* about something is to come straight out with your opinion, without worrying that you might offend someone. Presumably the things you are not fussing about are the other person's feelings.

'Break a leg'

Theatre people are notoriously superstitious and, just as it upsets them to mention *Macb*th* by name, so they wouldn't dream of wishing someone luck before a performance. So they say 'Break a leg' instead. There are many, many explanations for this choice of phrase, two of the more fanciful being anecdotes about John Wilkes Booth (said to have broken his leg jumping onto the stage of Ford's Theater after assassinating President Abraham Lincoln) and the famously one-legged actress Sarah Bernhardt.

A more probable theory is that the expression comes not originally from the theatre but from horse-racing. A horse breaking a leg would be the worst thing that could happen and making such a wish is, therefore, a sort of reverse psychology. The other plausible suggestion is that *to break a leg* is an old American idiom meaning much the same as TO BUST A GUT – in acting terms, to really go for it, to give an exhilarating performance.

Date? Difficult to be sure, but probably early-to-mid-twentieth century, and in the USA before the UK.

To break the bank

What every gambler in a casino longs to do, and what a certain Charles Deville Wells did in Monte Carlo in 1891: win more money than the bank is able to pay out. Wells was a con man on a grand scale, but there is no suggestion that he cheated at roulette – merely that he defrauded lots of people in order to have the money to gamble in the first place.

Nowadays, the expression is likely to be used in a negative sense and with a less exciting nuance: 'That won't break the bank' tends to mean nothing more interesting than 'I can afford it.'

To break the ice

A useful activity at parties or at potentially tricky meetings, this means to get the conversation going, to say something to make people feel more comfortable. Literally, of course, it means 'to forge a path through ice' and in this sense it is found in the sixteenth century. Francis Bacon's essay 'Of Cunning' (1597) has one of the first recorded idiomatic uses: advising on the tricks of persuasive argument, Bacon suggests breaking off in the middle of what

47

you are saying so that your listener is agog to know more; luring people in to ask you questions, so that they will be interested in your reply; and 'In things that are tender and unpleasing, it is good to break the ice by some whose words are of less weight, and to reserve the more weighty voice to come in, as by chance.' There are no inverted commas, no aside of 'as the saying is', indicating that the expression must already have been familiar.

To give someone a break

In the nineteenth century in the UK, a break was a collection made on behalf either of a prisoner awaiting trial (to help pay for his defence) or of one about to be released (so that he had some money to make a new start). This may be the origin of this expression, meaning to give someone a chance or, more recently, to get off their back, to stop nagging them. Alternatively, it may come from 'break' in the sense of 'an opportunity, a piece of good luck' – as in the actor W. C. Fields' cynical maxim 'Never give a sucker an even break.' It originated in the USA in the early part of the twentieth century and became widespread after Fields used his catchphrase as the title of a 1941 film.

A bridge too far

This was the name of a 1977 action film that (if you are old enough to have been watching action films at the time) starred almost everyone you'd ever heard of: Sean Connery, Michael Caine, Laurence Olivier, Gene Hackman, Robert Redford … It was based on a 1974 book of the same name by Cornelius

Ryan and concerned Operation Market Garden, an Allied initiative during the Second World War when troops were parachuted into the Netherlands with the mission to capture eleven bridges and secure a route into Germany. The film's script, written by the great William Goldman, includes a terribly British exchange when a corporal offers Major-General Urquhart (Sean Connery) a mug of tea.

'Hancock,' splutters Sean. 'I've got lunatics laughing at me from the woods. My original plan has been scuppered now that the jeeps haven't arrived. My communications are completely broken down. Do you really believe any of that can be helped by a cup of tea?'

'Can't hurt, sir,' comes the reply, and Sean accepts his tea.

Anyway, before all this, it is alleged that there was disagreement among the senior officers. Lieutenant-General Browning suggested to Field-Marshall Montgomery that the eleventh target might be 'a bridge too far'. It turns out he was right: the last part of the operation, at Arnhem, goes badly awry, only 2,000 of Urquhart's 35,000 men escape, and the expression has gone into the language to describe a drastic step or action that is likely to end in disaster.

To bring home the bacon

This expression has two related meanings: to earn money, particularly in the sense of having to make a living; and to succeed. There are complicated and conflicting explanations of its origins. A side of bacon known as the Dunmow Flitch ('flitch' being another word for a side of bacon and Great Dunmow being a place in Essex) was for hundreds of years the prize in a competition for married couples who could prove they had not had a cross word in the previous year. The winner literally *brought home the bacon*. Alternatively, 'bacon' was eighteenth-century thieves' slang for a prize or the loot.

Both these explanations are British-based, which makes it strange that the idiom should have been popularized in the USA in the early twentieth century. In 1906 boxer Joe Gans defeated 'Battling' Oliver Nelson to take the World Lightweight Championship. Before the fight Joe's mother sent him a telegram saying, 'Joe, the eyes of the world are on you. Everybody says you ought to win. Peter Jackson will tell me the news and you bring home the bacon.' An extravagant way of expressing herself, given that telegrams charged by the word, but the phrase seems to have taken off as a result.

To go for broke

This comes from a usage associated with the dice game of craps, popular in Hawaii in the early 1940s. Committed players knew that there was a moment when the game ceased to be a game and became something more serious than that. *To go for broke* meant to risk everything on the next roll of the dice.

At the time of the Japanese attack on Pearl Harbor (1941, which brought the United States into the Second World War), Hawaii was the home of a large number of Americans of Japanese descent. Anxious to show their loyalty to the country in which they now lived, they campaigned for the creation of a Japanese-American combat unit. In due course, and by special permission of President Roosevelt, the 442nd Infantry Regiment came into being. It chose as its motto 'Go for broke'. The American Army had the tact to post the unit to Europe (rather than the Japanese-dominated Pacific), where it fought with great gallantry and was much decorated.

Go for Broke was also the title of a 1951 film celebrating the regiment's achievements, and is now the name both of a monument to them in 'Little Tokyo' in Los Angeles and of a board game in which the aim is to spend as much money as possible in order to inherit a fortune. The latter does not seem to be exactly what the members of the 442nd had in mind when they chose their motto, but times change.

Brownie points

I've always thought this was an odd expression, because in the Brownies you don't get points, however well you behave: you get badges to show your ability in some specified activity such as cookery or stargazing. What's even odder is that

the phrase seems to have originated in the USA, where a brownie is a sort of chocolate cake and what in the UK is called a Brownie with a capital *B* is a Junior Girl Scout. But The Phrase Finder website reminds us of a third meaning of 'brownie': a benevolent elf or pixie (which is, by the way, where the Girl Scout-type of Brownie gets her name). It quotes from a 1951 article by Marvin Miles in *The Los Angeles Times*. *Brownie points*, he explains, are a way for a husband to assess the extent to which he is in his wife's bad books: 'Favor or disfavor. Started way back in the days of the leprechauns, I suppose, long before there were any doghouses.'

The problem with this is that elfish brownies belong to Scottish folklore, which takes them quite a distance from Los Angeles. In fact, nobody seems to be sure where the expression comes from, but I think the leprechaun explanation has decidedly more charm than the idea, which has also been suggested, that brownie points were army slang and you gained them by brown-nosing a senior officer.

To burn one's bridges

… or, in British English, *one's boats*: to commit oneself to a course of action so that there is no possibility of turning back. It's something Ancient Roman generals did, so that their troops couldn't take it into their heads to retreat. The idiomatic use dates from the late nineteenth century. And here's an instructive quotation from Tom Stoppard's *Rosencrantz and Guildenstern Are Dead* (1966): 'We cross our bridges when we come to them and burn them behind us, with nothing to show for our progress except a memory of the smell of smoke, and a presumption that once our eyes watered.'

Crossing your bridges when you come to them, of course, means not fretting about something until it occurs; once you have burnt them behind you it's too late to worry.

To burn the candle at both ends

This means to get up early and go to bed late, either to work or to party too hard. When Freddie Mercury of Queen fame died in 1991, his friend the DJ Kenny Everett reminisced about once going to a party at Freddie's house on a Saturday night and emerging on Tuesday morning: 'He burned the candle at both ends and in the middle, did Fred.'

When the expression came into being in the eighteenth century, however, this isn't what it meant

– *to burn a candle at both ends* was a sign of wanton extravagance, in the days when candles were a valuable resource. The traveller Jonas Hanway, in an account of British trade in the Caspian Sea, published in 1753, explained it as 'Apt to light their candle at both ends; that is to say, they are apt to consume too much, and work too little.'

That meaning was still current in 1920, when the poet and feminist Edna St Vincent Millay wrote:

> *My candle burns at both ends;*
> *It will not last the night;*
> *But ah, my foes, and oh, my friends –*
> *It gives a lovely light!*

But some time in the twentieth century this sense faded away and was overtaken by the idea that if you *burn your candle at both ends* you will, one way or another, burn yourself out.

To bury the hatchet

To end a quarrel and agree not to refer to it again. In the seventeenth century it is recorded that Native Americans made this symbolic gesture as a sign of peace between two tribes. By 1796 the satirist John

Wolcot, also known as Peter Pindar, was using the expression in a non-literal sense – possibly because his biting lampoons of prominent figures caused many hatchets to be raised against him. It was said that, like many people who make their name poking fun at others, he was extremely sensitive 'and, brandishing a tomahawk, always himself shrank from a scratch'.

To bust a gut

A none-too-elegant expression meaning to make a strenuous effort. Around since the early twentieth century, it must originally have implied the sort of physical effort that might have ended in a rupture or hernia. See also 'BREAK A LEG'.

C

Cack-handed

A British expression meaning clumsy or inept and/or left-handed. 'Cack' is an obsolete word for 'excrement' and in the days before toilet paper it was common in many cultures to use the left hand for … Need I go on? Being left-handed has always come in for abuse, witness the words *sinister* in Latin and *gauche* in French.

And it isn't just Latin and French. The Bulgarians have a word *lefteren*, derived from 'left', which means malfunctioning or not fit for purpose; the Cantonese *zuo* means both 'left' and 'a nuisance'; the Brabant dialect of the Netherlands says 'You are wearing your sweater the left way' to mean you have put it on inside out, you idiot; and the Filipino word for left-handedness also implies marital infidelity.

So from having a left hand that was covered in s**t to being incompetent as a result was but a step. The expression dates from the mid-nineteenth century; it wasn't very polite then and it isn't very polite now.

To call someone's bluff

To challenge someone to carry out a promise, in order to prove them wrong or show that they are lying or boasting. This comes from the game of poker, where bluffing – giving your opponents to understand that your hand is better than it is – is a common tactic. If you *call someone's bluff* they are obliged to reveal their cards and, all too often, forfeit their stake. The expression, like poker itself, first appeared in the USA in the early-to-mid-nineteenth century.

A cat in hell's chance

Normally prefixed by *not*, this means 'no chance at all'. Grose's *Classical Dictionary of the Vulgar Tongue* (1785) gives a longer version: *no more chance than a cat in hell without claws*, which is 'said of one who

enters into a dispute or quarrel with one greatly above his match'. The origin seems to be military: a cat going to hell without its claws would, obviously, be entering a difficult situation without adequate weapons and a soldier doing the same thing would be, to employ another idiom, *on a hiding to nothing*. In the early twentieth century the expression was frequently shortened to *a cat's chance*; the *hell* was restored in about the 1950s. There are many variations on the theme of what has no chance in hell: I've always thought *a snowball's chance in hell* is particularly evocative.

To let the cat out of the bag

This graphic description of revealing a secret may be connected with the idea of *buying a pig in a poke*. From the fourteenth century 'poke' was (and still occasionally is) a sort of bag or sack (and a 'poke-ette' or 'pocket' a smaller version of it) and it was not unusual to carry an animal to market in one. A pig, with its pork-and-bacon potential, was a valuable animal, so worldly wisdom advised against buying a pig in a poke without checking the contents first: an unscrupulous vendor might have substituted a cat, which, if you were looking to fatten it up and eat it, was a much less worthwhile purchase. To buy a pig in a poke, therefore, was and is to buy something unseen and untested; *to let the cat out of the bag* was to reveal the secret so that the buyer was not conned after all.

The flaw in this story is that *to buy a pig in a poke* is recorded as early as 1530 and *to let the cat out of the bag* not until 1760, but no one has yet come up with a better explanation. The first recorded use is in *The London Magazine or Gentleman's Monthly Intelligencer*: in its 'Catalogue of Books, with Remarks' in April of that year a reviewer has this tart observation on *The Life and Adventures of a Cat* by someone called Mynors: 'We could have wished that the author had not *let the cat out of the bag* [their emphasis], for it is such a mad, ranting, swearing, caterwauling puss, that we fear no sober family will be trouble with her.' Sadly Amazon has no record of this publication, which sounds as if it would be a real page-turner. It's worth noting the way *to let the cat out of the bag* is emphasized, though, because it indicates that the expression was already in use but that the reviewer perhaps felt it was a bit beneath him. As indeed was the book he was reviewing.

In 2013 it was announced that the makers of Monopoly had decided to update the tokens used in the game and that the iron, a feature since the game's debut in the 1930s, would be dropped in favour of a cat, which would be 'more representative of today's Monopoly players'. Some 10 million people showed their approval of the change by clicking the 'like' button on Facebook. (Or perhaps it was the same ironing-hating cat lover 10 million times. Either way, they should surely get out more.) At least one newspaper article on the subject was headed 'Cat's out of the bag'.

To be caught red-handed

To be caught in the act of committing a crime or misdemeanour, particularly and literally one involving blood. From the earliest times (the fifteenth century in Scotland, as far as this expression is concerned) the crime didn't have to be murder or GBH; it was more likely to have been poaching: the blood would have belonged to a stag that had gored you in self-defence. The idiom gradually evolved to encompass a wider range of crimes and by the middle of the nineteenth century you could be *caught red-handed* with nothing more bloody than someone else's jewellery about your person.

Big cheese

Not so much a cheese as a chiz, from a Persian or Hindustani word for 'thing'. The expression *the real chiz,* meaning 'the real thing, the real deal' or just something extremely good, was common among English speakers in India in the days of the Raj and in due course drifted back to Britain with them. There seems about the same time also to have been a British English expression *that's the cheese* or *that's the Stilton,* meaning much the same thing. So it's not surprising that the two should have merged, and that the recognizable 'cheese' should have taken precedence over the less familiar 'chiz'.

All this is on the eastern side of the Atlantic; in the early twentieth century the expression crossed over to the USA and – perhaps predictably, in the land of the supersize – had *big* attached to it. Initially – in *The Unprofitable Servant*, an unfinished short story by O. Henry dated 1910 – the Big Cheese meant wealth and social success: a vaudeville dancer named Del Delano is said to have 'crawled from some Tenth Avenue basement like a lean rat and had bitten his way into the Big Cheese … He had danced his way into health (as you and I view it) and fame in sixteen minutes.' Within a couple of decades the meaning had evolved to its current one: an important person, the boss, particularly one who has a tendency to be pleased with himself, be driven around in stretch limos and make unreasonable demands on his underlings. No apologies for the sexism of that last sentence: big cheeses tend not to be female, although it is probably only a matter of time.

Cheesed off

There are lots of expressions meaning 'fed up, exasperated, bored' – *brassed off* and *browned off* being only two of the more printable ones. *Browned off* is early twentieth-century army – and later RAF – slang, perhaps referring to an old vehicle or plane that has gone rusty and therefore brown. *Brassed off* is also from the services but slightly later, Second World War vintage; it may also derive from metalwork that is past its prime. No one seems to know why cheese should be invoked in this context, but a 1943 book of service slang gives the helpful nuance that *cheesed off* is 'more than *brassed off*; yet not entirely *browned off*'. So we may not know where it comes from, but at least we can use it with precision.

A (or an old) chestnut

This is a derogatory term for a joke, excuse or subject that one has heard too many times before. It was inspired by a play called *The Broken Sword* by William Dimond, first performed in 1816. One character starts telling a story that involves a cork tree and another interrupts him with, 'A chestnut, Captain, a chestnut ... This is the twenty-seventh time I have heard you relate this story, and you invariably said, a chestnut, till now.'

Some eighty years later, an actor called William Warren, who had often appeared in *The Broken Sword*, was listening to the club bore recounting an all-too-familiar anecdote. The actor mumbled this line under his breath – but not so deeply under his breath that the rest of the table didn't hear it and spread news of the witticism all over town. Or so legend has it.

The legend would be more plausible if it wasn't dated at 1896 and the *OED*'s first citation at 1886, but nonetheless something of this sort must have happened. *The Broken Sword* was the sort of panned-by-the-critics melodrama that audiences loved, and it is perfectly probable that someone, somewhere, among the many thousands who had seen or been

involved with the play, used the line when being told an old, old story.

More recently, *old chestnut* has been taken up in a number of different ways. It is, for example, the name of a 'rich, ruby-coloured winter ale' from the Ramsbury Brewery in Wiltshire and of an American film society dedicated to the showing of old-favourite movies. Both of these suggest an element of affection that was absent from the original quote and from the first uses of the idiom.

To have a chip on one's shoulder

A chip in this expression is a small block of wood, and the *Long Island Telegraph* of 20 May 1830 gives this explanation for its origins: 'When two churlish boys were *determined* to fight, a *chip* would be placed on the shoulder of one, and the other demanded to knock it off at his peril.' In other words, if you had a chip on your shoulder you were spoiling for a fight. The figurative meaning of 'to nurse a deeply engrained and usually irrational grievance' had established itself by the end of the nineteenth century.

Once an expression has become so well established as to be almost a cliché, it's not unusual for someone to play with it to make it sound more original. In the 1990s, for example, a disgruntled athlete sniped about a famous colleague that he was 'the most balanced runner in Britain because he's got a chip on both shoulders'.

As clean as a whistle

In 1828, one William Carr recorded this proverbial expression – meaning absolutely, perfectly clean – in *The dialect of Craven, in the West-Riding of the county of York*, but comparisons to a whistle go back further than that. Robert Burns's *The Author's Earnest Cry and Prayer* (1786), a heartfelt plea to the powers-that-be at Westminster not to put a high tax on Scottish whisky, contains the lines:

> *Paint Scotland greetin owre her thrissle;*
> *Her mutchkin stowp as toom's a whissle;*

This is, at a casual glance, Burns at his most demotic – or incomprehensible, if you prefer – but the second line translates as 'her three-quarter-pint drinking vessel as empty as a whistle'. Once you have it in plain English, this makes perfect sense, because a whistle has holes at both ends and on the side as well, so it would stay empty no matter how much whisky you poured into it.

So far so good, but why should a whistle be proverbial for its cleanliness? The best guess is that a brand-new whistle – straight out of the box, shiny and dirt-free – gives a pure, clean sound, which is adulterated as soon as the instrument becomes dusty or damp, or the holes are blocked. There may also be a connection with the fact that early, primitive whistles were whittled from a piece of wood, so that the original expression was *as clean as a whittle*. A whistle, or anything else, that had recently had its bark whittled away would display a clean, smooth surface. If this is the case the idiom is likely to have emerged in the American Wild West and have nothing to do with Rabbie Burns.

A clean sweep

Taken literally, this is what you get when you have used a broom thoroughly and removed the dust from all the corners; metaphorically, it refers to getting rid of everything unwanted from the old regime ('the new chairman made a clean sweep of the board of directors and brought in his own team') or to win every game in a contest ('the Czech team made a clean sweep of the gymnastics medals'). It's probably a spin-off from the proverb 'A new broom sweeps clean', which existed in the sixteenth century.

To take to the cleaners

You'd think this would be about making something squeaky clean, but no – *taking someone to the cleaners* is an underhand or fraudulent thing to do. It means defeating them soundly, probably *cleaning them out* of all their money. It is first found in the 1930s but remained distinctly North American for some time: the *Guardian* used it in 1961, but in inverted commas, which is shorthand for 'as the Americans say'.

The connection between money and cleaning took on a whole new lease of life at the time of the Watergate inquiry (1973–4), when the *Guardian* gave us the first mention of money being 'laundered' in Mexico. And lest there be any accusation of racism here, I should note that within a year or so the American *Publishers' Weekly* carried a report of money being 'laundered' in Switzerland; the Welsh-born but American-based novelist Jon Manchip White was pointing the finger at Phoenix, Arizona; and the Toronto *Globe and Mail* was suggesting that even Ontario wasn't, to mix a metaphor, squeaky clean. All these references put the word 'laundered' in inverted commas, as if the expression was a novelty, but – as anyone who has a bank account in the Cayman Islands knows – it has long since joined the mainstream.

The coast is clear

In Shakespeare's *Henry VI Part I* (*c*.1591), the Mayor of London disperses various lords who are fighting among themselves and then says to his own retinue, 'See the coast clear'd, and then we will depart.' He doesn't mean a literal coast – he means what we would mean if we said the same thing today – but when the expression was first recorded earlier in the sixteenth century a sea shore was actually involved. So if the coast was clear, there was no sign of the enemy (if you were at war) or the excisemen (if you happened to be a smuggler). The modern expression means 'It's OK, we can go', but still suggests we are doing something mildly nefarious.

(A load of) cobblers

Like TO BLOW A RASPBERRY, this is a not very elegant piece of Cockney rhyming slang. A cobbler works with an awl, a pointed tool for piercing leather: 'cobblers' awls' rhymes with 'balls', meaning

71

testicles, and *cobblers* is therefore a dismissive term for rubbish, nonsense. It's been around since the middle of the twentieth century and is one of many such expressions that are not as taboo as they once were because people have largely forgotten the origin.

To get cold feet

Ben Jonson's play *Volpone* (1605) refers to a Lombard proverb 'to have cold *on* one's feet', to be desperate for money, which is sensible enough:

if you're broke, you can't afford decent shoes. But the modern expression, meaning to take fright at a proposed course of action, to want to chicken out, doesn't seem to have evolved from this. No one seems entirely sure where it came from, but the same metaphor exists in German and the novelist Fritz Reuter used it in 1862 as the pretext for a card-player backing out of a game where the stakes had got too high. It is possible that his translator didn't recognize that it was an idiom, thought that the gambler really did want to leave the room because his feet were cold and rendered the words literally. Certainly it was established in American English by the end of the nineteenth century.

To give someone the cold shoulder

The Edinburgh-born novelist Sir Walter Scott (1771–1832) will make a number of appearances in this book, in this instance because it is likely that *to show* or *give someone the cold shoulder* is an expression he coined. It occurs in his *The Antiquary* (1816): 'The Countess's dislike didna gang farther at first than just showing o' the cauld shouther.' Scott's critics complained at his use of 'the dark dialect of Anglified Erse', but the author was ahead of them and had included a glossary in the first edition: here *to show the cauld shouther* is defined as 'to appear cold and reserved'. The form of words is almost certainly just a neater way of saying 'to turn one's back (or shoulder) coldly on someone'. If anything the meaning has become stronger over the years: *to give someone the cold shoulder* is not just to show coolness or disdain, but positively to rebuff them.

Cold turkey

Helping a drug user to stop using is often done by gradually lowering their intake so that they are eventually able to give up altogether, without too many horrific symptoms. Similarly, nicotine patches and the like are an aid to giving up smoking. The opposite technique is to go *cold turkey* – to give up, just like that, with no help, and to suffer the consequences.

The expression seems to be connected to *talking turkey* – originally *talking cold turkey* – which means to tell the unvarnished truth, to have an honest discussion. An early use, from the *Des Moines Daily News* of 1914, equates it with 'calling a spade a spade'. *To go cold turkey* might therefore have evolved because of its no-messing, let's-just-get-on-with-it approach. It's been around in North America since the 1920s and in the UK since at least the early 1960s.

John Lennon's Plastic Ono Band's second single was called 'Cold Turkey' and dealt with the horrors of coming off heroin. It peaked at a disappointing Number 14 in 1969 (their first single, 'Give Peace a Chance', had reached Number 2), then promptly slid down to 15. Three days later Lennon sent back to Buckingham Palace the MBE that he had been awarded four years earlier as a member of the Beatles, explaining, 'I am returning this MBE in protest against Britain's involvement in the Nigeria-Biafra thing, against our support of America in Vietnam, and against "Cold Turkey" slipping down the charts.' You could perhaps argue that this was *talking turkey*.

For another idiom with a token connection to the Beatles, see A DARK HORSE.

To cost an arm and a leg

To be extremely expensive, to cost more than most sensible people would be willing to pay. The expression dates from the middle of the twentieth century and is American in origin. There is no evidence for the commonly held view that it derives from a portrait painter charging more for a full-length portrait containing the sitter's arms and legs than for a mere head and shoulders. It's true – and surely not unreasonable – that large portraits were more expensive than small ones, but there is no evidence that Thomas Gainsborough or John Singer Sargent, for example, charged by the limb. If that had been the system, goodness knows how Salvador Dalí or Pablo Picasso would have worked out their price lists.

It's worth noting – should you be planning to go to France in the near future – that the equivalent French expression is 'to cost the eyes out of one's head' (*coûter les yeux de la tête*) or '… the skin off one's buttocks' (*la peau des fesses*) – again, drastic measures on the one hand, difficult pricing decisions for Dalí and Picasso on the other. See also TO GIVE ONE'S RIGHT ARM FOR.

Not all it's cracked up to be

In other words, not as good as popular report would have you think it was. One of the many meanings of 'to crack' is 'to boast, to talk big', so *to crack something up* is to praise it, possibly more than it deserves. 'Crack' in this sense is found in British English in the fifteenth century, but the idiom (originally *not all it's cracked up for*) emerged in the USA in the nineteenth and didn't make its way back across the Atlantic until well into the twentieth.

Crocodile tears

These are insincere tears or other expressions of grief or regret, derived from the ancient belief that crocodiles wept while devouring their prey. We now know that crocodiles do shed something that looks like tears, but this is only to lubricate their eyes after they have been out of the water for some time – as they may well be when they are feeding.

The idiom was in use by Shakespeare's time; although he doesn't use the exact words, he twice refers to the deception practised by lachrymose crocs. In *Henry VI Part II* we have:

Gloucester's show
Beguiles him as the mournful crocodile
With sorrow snares relenting passengers …

… and in *Othello*:

If that the earth could teem with woman's tears
Each drop she falls would prove a crocodile.

More recently *Crocodile Tears* has cropped up as the title of a song by Girls Aloud, referring to an insincere lover; and of one of Anthony Horowitz's novels about Alex Rider, teenage spy. The latter is set largely in East Africa and features real and rapacious crocodiles who don't seem to shed tears over anyone.

As I am writing this, an advertisement on the radio tells me – for some reason – that astronauts can't cry in space because there is no gravity. I don't know if this applies to crocodiles.

To cry over spilled milk

This expression, meaning belatedly to make a fuss about something you can do nothing about, is almost always found in the proverbial form *It's no use crying* … The exact wording has varied over the years – the milk may be shed rather than spilled and the crying may become weeping or sighing – but the concept is the same and has been around for almost four centuries: it's quoted in a 1659 book of British proverbs. It does, of course, advocate a philosophical approach to life, perhaps never more so than when Somerset Maugham wrote in *Of Human Bondage* (1915): 'It's no good crying over spilt milk, because all the forces of the universe were bent on spilling it.'

To cry wolf

This is that comparatively rare thing, an idiom whose origins we can pinpoint. It comes from the fable by Aesop, a Greek slave writing in the sixth century BC, who also gave us *sour grapes, slow and steady wins the race* and *don't count your chickens before they are hatched*.

The story goes that, in order to break the monotony of minding the sheep all day, a shepherd boy thought it would be fun to cry out, 'Wolf! Wolf!' The good folks in the village nearby came running to help, only to find themselves laughed at for being so easily duped. The boy did this again and again with the same result, so that when a wolf did appear and the lad cried for help, the neighbours would have none of it and the wolf destroyed the entire flock.

To cry wolf, therefore, is to call for help when it is not needed, with the result that no one believes you when you are telling the truth. And the moral is, obviously, 'Just don't do it.'

To curry favour

People who groom horses may use a currycomb to this day, and that is the meaning of 'curry' in this context – to groom a horse. It may also be applied to dressing leather after it has been tanned; it comes from an Old French word meaning 'to make ready' and has nothing to do with the spicy Indian dish.

So at first glance it would seem that the idiom began life meaning 'to groom or prepare favour', which would make some sort of sense, given the modern definition: 'to ingratiate oneself through grovelling behaviour or unnecessary attentions'. But in fact 'favour' here is a mishearing/misunderstanding/piece of folk etymology. The original expression was *to curry Fauvel,* Fauvel being the name of a fawn-coloured horse in a medieval French poem, *Le Roman de Fauvel.* The story goes that Fauvel, discontented with his quarters in the stables, moves himself to the best room of his master's house and there sets himself up as an important personage. Leaders of church and state promptly succumb to his self-mythologizing and come to suck up to him. It's worth noting – if you want to get the best out of this morality tale – that *fau vel* can be translated as 'veiled lie' and that the letters F-A-U-V-E-L are, in the French of the period, the initials of Flattery, Greed, Guile, Inconstancy, Envy and Cowardice. (We should be grateful that the story was written in French, because F-G-G-I-E-C doesn't spell out anything remotely improving.)

To return to our sheep, as the French would say, *to curry Fauvel* came to mean what it means today, but as time went by – and certainly by the early sixteenth century – someone thought, 'That can't

81

be right' and changed it to the current form. If you wondered earlier in the entry what folk etymology was, that is an example of it in practice – deciding that something can't be right and changing it to something that sounds better, but is wrong in terms of linguistic evolution.

English abounds with this sort of error: *spitting image*, for example, should really be *spit and image*, where 'spit' means an exact likeness, as if you had spat another person out of your mouth. But in some local dialects 'spit and' became 'spitten' and thence 'spitting'. 'Crayfish' comes ultimately from the Anglo-Norman *creveis* and was altered by someone who thought a crayfish was a fish; and 'female' derives from *femelle*, a diminutive of the French *femme*, altered by someone who wanted to make the connection with 'male'. See also TO EAT HUMBLE PIE.

To cut the mustard

To serve the purpose, to come up to expectation. Mustard is a condiment that adds piquancy to food and as such the word has been used since the seventeenth century, in expressions such as *as keen as mustard,* to indicate enthusiasm and verve. You can also *be the mustard* if you are just what the situation requires. But how and why should you cut it?

None of the explanations to do with the difficulty of cutting mustard seed (why would you bother?) or the densely growing mustard plant seem very plausible; nor does the idea that the expression somehow derives from the military concept of *mustering the troops* – *to pass muster* is a much older expression than *to cut the mustard*, which appears only in the late nineteenth century. The most likely answer is that mustard was seen as a good thing, a standard to which people aspired, and that 'cut' is used here in the same sense as *cutting a dash* or *cutting a caper* – performing or executing something with style. So it's like *passing muster* or coming UP TO SCRATCH, only rather better.

To cut to the chase

If you think of 'cutting' in the cinematic sense of 'moving to another part of the film' and of 'the chase' as 'the chase scene', you'll be there: skip the preliminaries, get on with the action or, in a broader sense, come straight to the point. The first (literal) use of the expression is credited to the early Hollywood scriptwriter J. P. McEvoy in 1929; it had assumed its current figurative meaning by the 1940s.

D

A dark horse

It's hardly surprising that this expression should have originated in horse-racing, but it's interesting that even in that milieu and from the word go it was figurative. The original *dark horse* wasn't necessarily dark in colour; it simply came like A BOLT FROM THE BLUE, astonishing everyone by streaking past the winning post. Perhaps the implication was that its owners and trainers had been keeping its talents dark.

This use dates from around the 1830s, and the idiom had moved away from horse-racing and into politics by the time the little-known James K. Polk was running for president of the United States in 1844: he was seen as a *dark horse* candidate who had yet to prove his worth, as indeed was Abraham Lincoln sixteen years later.

Dark Horse subsequently became the name of a record label founded by former Beatle George Harrison (and of an album he released on this label in 1974). Those who thought that he had written some decent songs but been unjustly overshadowed by Lennon and McCartney rather liked the combination of understatement and yah-boo-sucks that this implied. See also COLD TURKEY.

As dead as a doornail

A doornail is a stud set into a door to strengthen or decorate it; it may be that hammering it right through the door and then bending over the pointy end to give added strength meant that the nail was thereafter useless for anything else and thus 'deader' than any other kind of nail. Alternatively, the fact that another common expression for 'absolutely as dead as dead can be' is *as dead as a dodo* may suggest that – as in AS BOLD AS BRASS – alliteration is part of the explanation here.

Whatever the reasoning, *as dead as a doornail* is found as early as the mid-fourteenth century, and Shakespeare uses it without explanation in *Henry VI Part II* (1592), suggesting that it was well established in speech by then. In 1680 the dramatist Thomas Otway, in his play about the Roman general Marius, goes one (or two) further and describes someone as 'as dead as a Herring, Stock-fish, or Door-nail' – from which it seems safe to assume that he won't be coming back to haunt us any time soon.

Unlike, say, Marley in Dickens's *A Christmas Carol* (1843). The very first paragraph of the story tells us that Old Marley was 'as dead as a door-nail' and goes on to say:

> *Mind! I don't mean to say that I know, of my own knowledge, what there is particularly dead about a door-nail. I might have been inclined, myself, to regard a coffin-nail as the deadest piece of ironmongery in the trade. But the wisdom of our ancestors is in the simile; and my unhallowed hands shall not disturb it, or the Country's done for. You will therefore permit me to repeat, emphatically, that Marley was as dead as a door-nail.*

Marley, you may remember, did indeed come back to haunt Scrooge, giving the lie to all the author's scruples about respecting our ancestors.

A dead ringer

Originally American, a ringer is a person or thing that looks very like another and whose resemblance is often used for fraudulent purposes. The Phrase Finder quotes the *Manitoba Free Press* of October 1882 as explaining that 'a horse that is taken through the country and trotted under a false name and pedigree is called a "ringer".' But this is not the first appearance of the expression. Four years earlier, the *Weekly Register-call* of central Colorado was using it in the broader, modern sense: 'The knight of La Mancha storming a windmill, is a "dead ringer", so to speak, for Windy Bill riding down a phalanx of Mexicans on a long-eared mule.'

Twenty years before that, the word 'ringer' had been applied not to the phoney horse but to the person who practised the deception. The verb 'to ring' has meant 'to substitute one thing for another fraudulently' since the late eighteenth century and, although it is now rarely found in this sense, it is connected with TO RING THE CHANGES, which derives from a technical term used in bell-ringing. This may seem a long way from a fraudulent racehorse, but that is often the case with derivations.

As for 'dead', it is widely used to mean 'complete, absolute, utter' – *a dead loss, a dead certainty, dead centre, in deadly earnest* – and that is the sense here.

The expression has been a popular choice as a title for thrillers: Bette Davis starred in a 1964 film called *Dead Ringer*, in which a woman murders her wealthy twin sister and assumes her identity; in 1988 David Cronenberg directed *Dead Ringers*, about two twin brothers, both gynaecologists, who use the fact that no one can tell them apart to take advantage of their patients; and 'Dead Ringer' is also the title of a 2004 episode of *CSI: Crime Scene Investigation*, in which one of the several murder victims is suspected of being a ringer in a long-distance relay race. The rock singer Meatloaf had a hit in the 1980s with 'Dead Ringer for Love', but as this includes the line 'I'm looking for anonymous and fleeting satisfaction', it may be that the word 'love' in the title is intended to be satirical.

What the dickens?

'Speak of the devil and he will appear,' goes the old saying, and this expression bears that in mind. *What the devil?* – like 'What on earth?' or 'What in heaven's name?' – is merely an emphatic way of asking 'What?', and *What the dickens?* makes the same point without the risk of summoning up the Prince of Darkness. It's nothing to do with the novelist Charles (Shakespeare used it in *The Merry Wives of Windsor* over 200 years before Dickens was born); and may be a corruption of 'devilkin' or little devil.

Having said the expression was nothing to do with Charles Dickens, I can't resist mentioning that in the 1960s the great jazz musician John Dankworth recorded an album called *What the Dickens!* which included the tracks 'Please Sir, I Want Some More', 'Waiting for Something to Turn Up', 'The Artful Dodger' and 'The Pickwick Club'. You somehow can't see a twenty-first-century boy band doing that, can you?

To go to the dogs

Similar in meaning to TO GO TO POT, this is to deteriorate, to suffer a decline in standards, to start leading a shameful life. In British English 'to go to the dogs' means literally to attend a greyhound race meeting, but this practice has been around only for a hundred years or so – the metaphorical concept of *going to the dogs* pre-dates it by some three centuries.

There are two possible explanations. One, that anything in the food line that was unfit for human consumption was given to the dogs; the other that in Ancient China dogs were not permitted within the city walls and therefore roamed around outside them. Anyone who was exiled was therefore deemed to have *gone to the dogs*, in that they would henceforth share the dogs' territory and, like them, scavenge a living as best they could.

The expression was well into the realms of cliché when Dorothy L. Sayers used it in *Unnatural Death* (1927). A village publican is explaining how the local hunt had met less regularly, 'owing to the War and the gentlemen being away and the horses too':

> *But what with the foxes gettin' so terrible many, and the packs all going to the dogs – ha! ha! – that's what*

*I often used to say in this bar – the 'ounds is goin'
to the dogs, I says. Very good, they used to think it.
There's many a gentleman has laughed at me sayin'
that – the 'ounds, I says, is goin' to the dogs.*

AN OLD CHESTNUT, would you say?

Double whammy

*Evil-Eye Fleagle had a unique and terrifying skill.
When he concentrated, destructive rays emitted from
his eyeballs. An ordinary 'whammy' could knock a
grown man senseless. A 'double whammy' could fell a
skyscraper, leaving Evil-Eye exhausted. His dreaded
'quadruple whammy' could melt a battleship.*

So runs the description on YouTube accompanying
a brief clip of Evil-Eye destroying a solid wall with
the mere power of his glance. A character from the
comic strip *Li'l Abner*, created by Al Capp in the
1930s, he is apparently based on a real-life boxing
manager called Benjamin 'Evil Eye' Finkle, who
had a reputation for putting a hex on his fighters'
opponents. Capp may not have invented the
concept of the *whammy* – it appears in a baseball
novel by John R. Tunis around the same time – but

91

Evil-Eye Fleagle certainly brought it to a very wide public.

Thus a *whammy* came to mean any powerful blow or setback, and a *double whammy* meant two such unpleasant occurrences coming along at once. In the USA the expression was initially confined to the world of sport; in the UK it came to prominence during the 1992 general election, when the Conservative Party's campaign included a poster featuring a large pair of boxing gloves, one labelled '1. More Taxes' and the other '2. Higher Prices'. Above the image was the slogan (said to have been the brainwave of Chris Patten, then Chairman of the Conservatives) 'Labour's Double Whammy' – a dire warning of what would happen if too many people voted for the Opposition party. They didn't, on that occasion, but whether or not that was in reaction to the poster is difficult to assess.

Down in the dumps

There is a story – put about by the eighteenth-century poet John Gay – that Dumops was an Egyptian king who died of melancholy and that 'dumps' is a corruption of his name. This is no more true than the idea, also Gay's, that the word 'mope' derives from an Egyptian king called Merops, but you can't help admiring the man who made it up.

In fact, a 'dump' has, since the sixteenth century, been 'a fit of abstraction, absence of mind' and thence (and often in the plural, as it is today) 'a fit of melancholy or depression'. *Down in the dumps* first appears in print in Grose's *Dictionary of the Vulgar Tongue* (1785) and has been in constant use ever since. The great blues singer Bessie Smith had a hit with a song of this name in 1933, but then 'Down in the Dumps' could probably be the title, or at least the subtitle, of any blues song ever written.

Down to earth

Practical and realistic, with no pretensions or flights of fancy. The *OED*'s first recorded use – from P. G. Wodehouse's *Very Good, Jeeves* (1930) – is 'I had for some little time been living, as it were, in another world. I now came down to earth with a bang.' Other uses about this time put the words *down to earth* in inverted commas, suggesting that they are a novelty, so it is quite possible that Wodehouse invented the expression as the obvious comeuppance for anyone who had been foolish enough to be living in another world. Even if he didn't, he almost certainly added

to it. Nowadays *I came down to earth with a bang* would be a commonplace thing to say, but Wodehouse never wrote a commonplace phrase in his life, so it is very likely that he was the first person to come up with that particular combination.

Down to the wire

Used to describe a decision that isn't made or a situation that isn't resolved until the very last moment, this is another expression from American horse-racing (see, for example, HANDS DOWN, BY A LONG SHOT and NECK AND NECK). In the late nineteenth century a wire was strung across the track above the finishing line – high enough above it that the horses didn't run into it, one assumes – to help stewards decide who was the winner. Thus a race that went *down to the wire* was what later, when the technology came along, was described as *a photo finish*.

The expression has broadened in its use to the extent that a 2006 report on Formula One racing could refer to the championship going *down to the wire* – in a sport where wire across the track has never been official and could potentially be fatal.

To draw a blank

In Elizabethan times, a lottery involved writing the ticket-holders' names on slips of paper and putting them into one pot; then writing the prizes on other slips of paper and putting them into another pot.

As there were, of course, fewer prizes than there were participants, the contents of the second pot were bulked up with blanks. Slips were then drawn alternately from each pot. If, after your name was drawn, the slip from the other pot was a blank, you lost.

One of the many meanings of the verb 'to draw', also dating from Elizabethan times, is 'to search a wood or covert for game'. Somehow these two uses became confused, so that by the nineteenth century, in hunting circles, *to draw a blank* also meant to find nothing after a rigorous search. From gambling and hunting, the expression has expanded to describe any unsuccessful enterprise or downright failure.

Back to the drawing board

A fairly obvious one, this: a drawing board is something on which, in pre-computer days, an architect or designer would draw plans. If, once a building went on site, it seemed likely to fall down, or if a dress didn't hang the way it should, it would have to be re-thought out and the plans redrawn. Hence, *back to the drawing board*.

The idiom is one of those rare ones whose origins can be firmly pinned down (see TO CRY WOLF for another). It was first used in a cartoon by Peter Arno in *The New Yorker* of 1 March 1941: a designer, with a roll of plans under his arms, is seen walking away from a plane crash. The caption reads, 'Well, back to the old drawing board.'

The sense quickly broadened to apply to any design or plan that has gone awry. The Phrase Finder quotes an American football report from 1947: 'Grid injuries for the season now closing suggest anew that nature get back to the drawing board, as the human knee is not only nothing to look at but also a piece of bum engineering.' That's using the word 'bum' in the American sense, not the British one, of course.

To drive someone nuts/to drive someone round the bend

'To drive' in the sense of 'to force into a condition' has been around since the thirteenth century and coupled with an adjective such as 'mad' or 'crazy' since the early nineteenth. *Nutty* or *nuts* meaning insane or eccentric can be traced to the late nineteenth-century USA: if you accept that 'nut' means head, as it has (probably because of its shape) since the early nineteenth century, then to be *off one's nut* is to be out of one's mind, and *nutty* and *nuts* follow easily from there. *To drive someone nuts* is an obvious combination of the two ideas.

To drive someone round the bend requires more thought. Suggestions that, in some unspecified olden days, mental asylums were hidden from the road by a bend in the driveway or, alternatively, accessed round a certain bend in a river, seem to have no evidence to back them up. More credible is a 1929 source that describes the phrase as 'old naval slang' and suggests that it is somehow connected with knots (a bend is a knot used for tying two ropes together or for tying a rope to something else) and possibly with another word for mildly insane: *loopy*. Remembering my time in the Girl Guides, I can imagine that spending your time mastering lots of knots could drive anyone round the bend. Or nuts.

At the drop of a hat

This is a mixture of 'immediately' and 'at the slightest provocation, without any real reason', as in 'She's likely to burst into tears at the drop of a hat.' It seems to have originated in the Wild West, where dropping a hat was the signal for a boxing or wrestling match to begin.

If you are old enough to remember Michael Flanders and Donald Swann, you will need no reminding that their first revue together was called *At the Drop of a Hat*. They described their performance as 'an after dinner farrago' (no hyphen? In those days? Shocking!) and the programme for their first night – New Year's Eve 1956 – is a perfect example of the use of the expression. It reads: 'At the drop of a hat, Michael Flanders & Donald Swann will perform – regardless.' To hear them singing the

praises of London Transport's 'ninety-seven horse-power omnibus', practising the art of seduction with the offer 'Have some Madeira, m'dear' or sharing the delights of the hippopotamus wallowing in 'mud, mud, glorious mud' would have cost you anything from 17½p to 52½p. What a night that must have been.

To drum up

One of the definitions of 'to drum' is 'to summon by or as if by the beat of a drum'; Shakespeare uses this in *Antony and Cleopatra* (*c*.1606). From this, by the middle of the nineteenth century, came the colloquial *to drum up*, to obtain something by canvassing or soliciting, as in *to drum up trade* or *to drum up votes*. There are a number of other things that can be done to the beat of a drum, such as being *drummed out of town* or *drummed out of the regiment*. This last sense, dating from the eighteenth century, describes someone being disgraced, the noise of the drum doubtless intended to draw attention to the fact and heighten their embarrassment. You can also, of course, if you are an old-fashioned sort of teacher, *drum* information *into* your pupil (nineteenth century) by repeating it over and over again, as if to the repetitive rhythm of a drum beat.

To go Dutch

The English/British were at war with the Dutch off and on throughout the seventeenth century and again towards the end of the eighteenth. All sorts of expressions derogatory to the Netherlanders came into being at that time. The wonderfully disdainful *Dutch nightingale*, meaning a frog, sadly seems to have passed into oblivion, as does *a Dutch bargain*, one made over a drink or three. But we still have *Dutch comfort* – not really comfort at all – and the rather old-fashioned *to talk to someone like a Dutch uncle*, to berate them.

The nineteenth century saw a large wave of immigration from the Netherlands to the USA, where – perhaps because they were economic migrants who had spent most of their savings getting there – the Dutch earned a reputation for being, shall we say, careful with their money. Thus in the early part of the twentieth century we find the concept of a *Dutch lunch* or *Dutch treat*, in which everyone pays their own way: that is, they *go Dutch*.

It's worth noting that the English language has always had an open-handed approach to the abuse of foreigners, particularly when it comes to matters sexual. Syphilis has at various times been termed the *French* or the *Spanish pox* or the *Neapolitan disease*; *French letters* and *French safes* (different words for the same thing) appeared in fashionable London in the mid-nineteenth century; and we even once had an unappetizing-sounding dish, half a sheep's head boiled with onions, which we called *German duck*. You'd need a certain amount of *Dutch courage* to get through a helping of that.

E

To eat one's hat

This is what you promise to do if something really improbable happens: 'if X wins the election/passes his exams/turns up on time, I'll eat my hat.' Thomas Bridges uses the expression in 1797 in *Homer Travestie*, a burlesque translation of Homer's *Iliad*.

> *I'll eat my hat, if Jove don't drop us,*
> *Or play some queer rogue's trick to stop us.*

It's clear from this, though, that this is a recognized idiom, so while the prospect of eating something unpleasant and difficult to chew may not be as old as the Trojan War, it still dates back further than 1797.

A different form of the expression had appeared at least another hundred years earlier, in the time of Charles II (1660–85), who was sometimes nicknamed Old Rowley. *I'll eat Old Rowley's hat* meant exactly the same as the current expression; The Phrase Finder points out that His Majesty favoured a large and florid form of headgear that would have been even more difficult to eat than yours or mine. To say nothing of the fact that you would probably have found yourself in the Tower if you tried to get hold of it.

Bridges, by the way, didn't want anyone to miss out on the fact that his translation was a send-up of the original: he published it under the nom de plume of Caustic Barebones.

To egg someone on

Nothing to do with the sort of eggs you scramble or fry, this comes from an Old Norse word *eggja*, meaning 'to incite'. Old Norse was introduced to the British Isles by the Viking invaders, who weren't known for holding back, so this was probably a word the invadees heard a lot. At first you would simply be *egged* to do something; *egging on* came in in the sixteenth century, but both mean the same thing.

To make ends meet

Many people will be familiar with the concept of there being too much month left at the end of the money; if you can just about make your salary last until the next pay cheque comes along, you are *making ends meet*. But ends of what?

One explanation is that the phrase is short for *to make the two ends of the year meet,* meaning to make the books tally, to have the column recording income equal the one recording expenditure. But this form is first recorded in the eighteenth century, by which time *to make both ends meet* had been around for nearly a hundred years.

This makes the alternative explanation perhaps more probable: that it comes from dress-making, with the understanding that a piece of cloth is cut generously enough to wrap around the body – but only just; in the budget of someone struggling to make ends meet, there is no scope for generous draping.

Nowadays it is all too common for the expression to be prefixed by *struggling* or some other such problematic word, as when the American comedian Allan Sherman (1924–73) complained, 'I was having trouble making ends meet, and my beginnings weren't meeting either.'

F

To face the music

'Origin uncertain and disputed,' says the *OED*, and certainly it isn't easy to imagine why facing up to something unpleasant should be associated with an art form that most people find agreeable. Making a nervous cavalry horse face the military band, drumming someone out of the regiment (see TO DRUM UP) or forcing a nervous actor to face the orchestra – and therefore the audience – have all been suggested, but none seems to be based on any more evidence that the others. Early nineteenth-century American is all we can say for sure.

The expression was familiar enough in the 1930s for Irving Berlin to use it twice – *Face the Music* is the title of a musical comedy about a group of theatrical impresarios struggling to cope with the deprivations of the Depression and, perhaps more famously, 'Let's Face the Music and Dance' is a song from the film *Follow the Fleet*. In this, Fred Astaire and Ginger Rogers proved – as so often – that facing the music (or facing away from the music or facing in who cares what direction?) and dancing was what they did best.

Fagged out

An early British meaning of 'to fag' is 'to flag' (from which it may derive), 'to droop or decline'. From this, by the eighteenth century, it came to mean to do something exhausting or to be exhausted by something ('It fags me to work all day'). Thence *to be fagged* was to be very tired and *fagged out* is found by the middle of the nineteenth century. The public schoolboy who toasts crumpets for prefects is connected with this meaning and is found as early as 1785.

By a different path, but still connected with drooping, comes a 'fag-end', the last part of a piece of cloth, often coarser than the rest, and also the untwisted end of a piece of rope, with spare strands hanging down. Metaphorically a 'fag-end' quickly came to mean the last, fading-away part of anything (the fag-end of a leg of mutton, of a hurricane and of a Parliament are all found in the seventeenth century) and from this sense comes the fag-end or 'fag' of a cigarette, thence a cheap cigarette and in due course any cigarette at all.

Fair and square

A square is (as the dictionaries put it) rectilinear, with sides of the same length, held together by right angles, all very accurate and, well, square. So it isn't surprising to find a metaphorical meaning – accurate, honest, ABOVE BOARD – from early on. *Square dealing* and *square play* occur in the sixteenth and seventeenth centuries; Shakespeare used 'square' on its own in this sense more than once and as recently as the 1950s, in the film *Gentlemen Prefer Blondes,* the boyfriend Marilyn Monroe was leaving behind as she travelled to Europe was urging her to 'write and declare/That though on the loose/You are still on the square'. Fat chance, you might think, but that needn't concern us here.

Another word for accurate, honest and above board, of course, is 'fair' and pairing the two to make a neat, rhyming, trip-off-the-tongue expression was not long in coming: Francis Bacon did it while

Shakespeare was still sharpening his quill. Latterly Michelle Obama has told us that 'success doesn't count unless you earn it fair and square', though the cynics among us may beg to differ.

A far cry (from)

Not many people read Sir Walter Scott nowadays, but there's no denying he's a useful source of material for books like this: tinyonline.co.uk rightly describes him as 'that great reviver of rustic phrases and inventor of new ones'. And here he is in action.

In the days before telephones, a place that was 'within call, within cry' was near enough that they could hear you if you yelled. Self-evidently, the further away the place was, the louder you had to shout. Scott, writing in *A Legend of Montrose* (1819), says, 'One of the Campbells replied, "It is a far cry to Lochow"; a proverbial expression of the tribe, meaning that their ancient hereditary domains lay beyond the reach of an invading enemy.' Did Scott make it up? Was it genuinely a proverbial expression of the Campbells? Who knows? But that is where it comes from.

From there it was but a short step to making *a far cry* not only distant but different. By 1885 the literary magazine *Athenaeum* was able to observe, 'It is a far cry from the ascidian to bookbinding and blue china' and, whether or not you dash to the dictionary to look up 'ascidian'[1], there is no arguing with that.

On the first page of Muriel Spark's novel *A Far Cry from Kensington* (1988), the narrator lies awake at night and revels in the silence – *a far cry*, she thinks, from the rowdy Kensington boarding house of her 1950s youth. Which suggests that 1950s Kensington was *a far cry* from the wealthy, Chelsea-tractor-ridden enclave it is today.

In fine fettle

As far back as 1400, and still today in some parts of the world, 'to fettle' means to tidy up, to put in order and specifically to groom a horse or attend to cattle. By the eighteenth century the verb had

---

[1] It's a member of a group of animals belonging to the tunicate Mollusca, considered by evolutionists to constitute a link in the development of the Vertebrata, and if there are several words in that definition that you feel the need to look up, you're on your own.

become a noun and one could be *in good* or *bad fettle*, or just *in fettle*, meaning young, fit, healthy and full of the joys of spring. *Fine fettle*, with its alliterative attraction, came along towards the end of the nineteenth century.

A fish out of water

… will be very uncomfortable and in due course will drown. That's the figurative meaning of the expression, too.

The idea has been around since at least the fourteenth century, when Chaucer used it in the Prologue to *The Canterbury Tales*:

... a monk, when he is cloisterless;
Is like to a fish that is waterless

... and 600 years later it was still good enough for Dolly Parton. Her 1992 song 'Fish out of Water' includes the words 'out of my element' and 'flounderin' round' – precisely what a fish out of water does.

As fit as a fiddle

Alliteration again (see, for example AS BOLD AS BRASS and AS DEAD AS A DOORNAIL): there's no reason why a fiddle should be fitter than anything else, but you can't deny it sounds right. The fact that people also used to say *as fine as a fiddle* adds weight to this argument. 'Fit' in the early days (seventeenth century or so) meant not 'hale and hearty' but 'appropriate, fit for purpose' (as in 'a fit companion'), but that comes no closer to explaining why a fiddle should have been chosen as the exemplar of fitness.

Other now-obsolete expressions merely add to the confusion: to have *a face as long as a fiddle* meant to look sorrowful, while *to have one's face made of a fiddle* meant to be charming. Perhaps people admired the fiddle because it produced lively music that required great skill to play. Or perhaps they just liked the sound of the word.

A flash in the pan

Unless you're a firearms enthusiast you've probably never seen a flintlock in action. It ceased to be state-of-the-art in the gun world about 200 years ago. But the way it worked was that pulling the trigger caused the hammer to strike a flint. This in turn produced a spark that ignited the gunpowder, which was stored in a compartment known as a pan. If the flint produced the spark but the gunpowder failed to ignite, the result was *a flash in the pan*.

Figuratively, the expression describes anything that has a brief period of success but no lasting impact. Writing around 1900 in 'Extradited from Bohemia', about characters eager to make their mark in New York's art world, the American master of the short story O. Henry describes a restaurant where these people hang out:

> *The room was full of the fragrance of flowers – both mille and cauli. Questions and corks popped; laughter and silver rang; champagne flashed in the pail, wit flashed in the pan …*

… and, we can safely assume, no one ever achieved lasting success.

Fly-by-night

Grose's *Classical Dictionary of the Vulgar Tongue* (1785) tells us that *fly-by-night* is 'an ancient term of reproach to an old woman, signifying that she was a witch'. Certainly its original meaning was literal – 'one who flies by night', which in human terms can only have been a witch. From there it quickly developed to mean someone who disappeared (without actually flying) by night, usually omitting to pay the rent.

Fly-by-night can also now be an adjective, describing not only a person but a thing. The Brighton Pavilion website tells an engaging story of a sedan chair on wheels, designed in the early nineteenth century, when 'fly' was a name for a small one-horse carriage. These sedans became popular with the Prince Regent and his rowdy chums and 'from being employed by them on special occasions of a midnight "lark", they received the name "Fly-by-nights".'

113

With flying colours

A ship's colours are its flags, which indicate the country it's from and what sort of vessel it is. Regiments have colours, too, and soldiers going into battle or on parade used to march behind them. *To come off with flying colours,* therefore, whether you were a ship or a soldier, meant to emerge from battle with your banner intact – a sure indication of victory. As early as the seventeenth century the idea was extended to describe success in any venture.

To sail under false colours (deliberately to misrepresent oneself and one's motives), *to nail one's colours to the mast* (to leave others in no doubt about one's allegiance) and *to show one's true colours* (to reveal one's true nature or intentions, particularly if they are unpleasant) all refer to this sense of the word *colours.*

To foam at the mouth

A dog with rabies foams at the mouth because the rabies virus produces an excess of saliva. Shakespeare used the expression in 1599, when he had Julius Caesar faint in the marketplace: he 'foamed at the mouth and was speechless'. Modern medical opinion differs as to what Caesar's problem was – it is traditionally but not necessarily accurately said to have been epilepsy – but there is no doubt that Shakespeare was describing a literal, physical symptom. A century later the essayist Richard Steele wrote of 'foaming at the mouth and acting a sort of madness' – so that *foaming at the mouth* came to mean being prey to an uncontrollable emotion. Nowadays, to our shame, that uncontrollable emotion is almost always rage.

To put one's foot in it

To make an embarrassing or tactless mistake, as exaggerated by the old joke, 'Every time I open my mouth I put my foot in it.' For some reason, in early uses of this expression, the blunder was attributed to a bishop: if milk or soup was burned, it was proverbially said – in the sixteenth century – that 'the bishop hath set his foot in it'. The pioneering translator of the Bible William Tyndale (*c*.1494–1536) gives – in *The Obedience of a Christian Man* (1528) – the macabre explanation that this was because bishops had a habit of burning anyone or anything that displeased them. By the nineteenth

century, when burning heretics had gone out of fashion, the expression had been simplified to its current form.

Forty winks

To have (or *take* or occasionally *catch*) *forty winks* means to take a brief nap, perhaps after lunch, and probably on the sofa or in an armchair rather than in bed – but why winks, and why forty?

The most likely explanation is that a wink is the shortest possible length for a bit of 'shut-eye' – it's over *in the blinking of an eye*, to use a related idiom. On the other hand, 'forty' is traditionally used to mean 'an unspecified but large number', as in the biblical 'forty days and forty nights' and the boast of Shakespeare's Coriolanus that 'On fair ground I could beat forty of them.' So *forty winks* would be 'quite a lot of very little sleeps'.

An early use of the expression appears in the USA in 1821 in Dr William Kitchiner's immensely popular self-help guide *The Art of Invigorating and Prolonging Life*. '"A Forty Winks Nap",' he writes, 'in an horizontal posture, is the best preparative for any extraordinary exertion of either [the body or the mind].' Half an hour is specified as the ideal length for this nap. It's noticeable, however, that Dr Kitchiner puts 'Forty Winks Nap' in inverted commas, suggesting that he is quoting rather than coining the phrase.

On the other side of the Atlantic, we find a *Punch* journalist in 1872 satirizing the dreariness of the Thirty-Nine Articles, which outline the doctrine of the Church of England; he suggests that no blame would attach 'if a man after reading through the Thirty-Nine Articles, were to take forty winks'. But here again it's clearly an established phrase being given a new twist.

To have a frog in one's throat

Frogs are croaky; if you have a cold or something else that makes you speak hoarsely, you sound croaky, too. Put the two together and it's easy to see where this image comes from. It seems to have originated in the USA in the mid-nineteenth century. A clergyman named Harvey Newcomb, in an improving book called *How to Be a Man* (1847), advised his young readers to resist the temptation of 'improper diversions' (the mind boggles) by saying no to them. He continued, 'If you find a *"frog in your throat,"* which obstructs your utterance, go by yourself, and practise *saying* no, no, NO!' Clearly the expression was already known by the time Harvey wrote it down, but this is the first recorded use.

Harvey didn't restrict his advice to boys; in the same year he produced *How to Be a Lady*, which contains this gem for those who attend mixed-gender schools:

> … *the sports in which boys usually engage are improper for your sex; and for you to engage in rude, boisterous conversation and coarse jesting, such as ill-bred youth are wont to practise, would be highly unbecoming.*

That's ill-bred youth who haven't read the Reverend Harvey's book, of course.

Full of beans

Apparently if you feed horses on beans they become more lively and spirited, run faster and win you more money. Thus *to be full of beans* is to be enthusiastic and energetic. Appropriately, therefore, the earliest example of the expression was penned by the comic novelist R. S. Surtees, creator of the sporting-mad and endlessly enthusiastic John Jorrocks. ''Ounds, 'osses, and men, are in a glorious state of excitement! Full o' beans and benevolence!' cries the Cockney Mr Jorrocks in *Handley Cross* (1843), having somehow become Master of the Surrey Hounds.

This is another expression to be wary of, however, if you are crossing the Atlantic. In the USA 'beans' may be used as a euphemism for something else that people are sometimes said to be full of. So saying to someone over breakfast, 'You're full of beans this morning' may not be as friendly as you intend it to be.

G

To give up the ghost

An early meaning of the word 'ghost' is the spirit or soul – hence the Christian Holy Ghost, now usually called the Holy Spirit. *To give up the ghost* is thus to give up the soul or, more simply, to die. It occurs in the Bible: Matthew's account of Christ's crucifixion has him *giving up the ghost*, according to the fourteenth-century Wycliff translation, though the King James version two and a bit centuries later has *yielded up the ghost*.

Over time the expression evolved so that it came to refer both to animals dying and to inanimate objects falling into a state of collapse. In 1879 a hunting memoir from Burma explained – with apparent approval – that 'a tiger ... shot through the heart ... is still capable of killing half-a-dozen men before giving up the ghost.' A couple of generations later priorities had changed for the upper classes: a character in P. G. Wodehouse's *Ring for Jeeves* (1953) explains that she had to cut her holiday short because 'my allowance met those New York prices and gave up the ghost with a low moan.'

The gift of the gab

A gift traditionally attributed to the Irish or to silver-tongued salespeople, this means the ability to talk with great fluency and plausibility, but not necessarily sincerity. 'To gab' is associated with 'to gabble' and seems originally to be Scottish; our expression is first recorded as *the gift of the gob* in 1695 and is recorded in its modern form in Grose's *Dictionary of the Vulgar Tongue* ninety years later.

The Irish connection is, of course, associated with kissing the Blarney Stone, which traditionally imparts the eternal gift of eloquence. Cormac MacDermott MacCarthy, who owned Blarney Castle, just outside Cork, in the time of Queen Elizabeth I, is said to have been the origin of the concept of 'Blarney talk'; he continually delayed swearing allegiance to Elizabeth, professing undying loyalty but fobbing her representative off with soft words. It is even said that Her Majesty, finally losing patience, made the first idiomatic use of Cormac's home: 'This is all Blarney, he never means what he says, and he never does what he promises.'

No one knows quite why kissing the Blarney Stone came to be a symbolic gesture, although the castle's website tells us that a witch saved from drowning

revealed its power to the MacCarthys. (Nonsense, of course, because everyone knows witches can't drown: that's why they used to burn them.) What we do know is that it is not for the faint-hearted: it requires you to lean backwards over a high parapet. In 1948 it was considered dangerous enough for a Sherlock Holmes story to feature a man who died from a fall there. The great detective discovered that it was a murder, because someone had greased the victim's boots to lessen his grip. Fear not, Health and Safety have left their mark since then. (Yes indeed, Arthur Conan Doyle did die in 1930 and never sent Sherlock Holmes within spitting distance of the Blarney Stone. It was a radio broadcast involving a bit of dramatic licence at the BBC.)

To gird up one's loins

To gird is to put a girdle or belt round your waist, tucking a long flowing garment into it to give yourself more freedom of movement; *girding up your loins* – for men in particular – suggests putting some of the garment between your legs and then tucking it into your belt. You might do it if you were getting down to some hard manual labour or setting out on a long walk or run. In the second Old Testament book of Kings, for example, God advises Gehazi, 'Gird up thy loins, and take thy staff in thine hand and go thy way.' The expression crops up a number of times in the Bible, including in the first letter of Peter, by which time it has moved into metaphor: 'Gird up the loins of thy mind, be sober, and hope to the end for the grace that is to be brought unto you at the revelation of Jesus Christ.' Both these expressions are found in the Coverdale translation of the Bible (1535) and the concept of girding oneself, if not specifically one's loins, is found in the Lindisfarne Gospels of AD 950.

The better part of a thousand years later, Walter Scott's romantic poem *The Lady of the Lake* (1810) has this stirring stuff:

> *The thunderbolt had split the pine, –*
> *All augured ill to Alpine's line.*
> *He girt his loins, and came to show*
> *The signals of impending woe.*

Read that without laughing if you can, but nowadays we do tend to use the expression in a jocular sense: 'I must gird my loins and go home', you might say at the end of a pleasant evening when the prospect of going out into the cold doesn't appeal.

To get someone's goat

Another Americanism, meaning to make someone very angry, to really touch a nerve – but why a goat? According to The Phrase Finder, an American book called *Life in Sing Sing,* published in 1904, says that 'goat' is a slang word for 'anger' and the expression is first recorded about this time. *Life in Sing Sing* is in fact one of a series published under the blanket title *Making of the Modern Law: Legal Treatises, 1800–1926* and containing essays by every legal theorist you have ever heard of and many more that you haven't. If they say that 'goat' means 'anger' and they have the inmates of Sing Sing to back them up, who am I to argue?

An alternative theory is that a goat was sometimes housed alongside a racehorse to keep the latter calm. Stealing the goat, therefore, would upset the horse. This seems to run contrary to the theory expressed in FULL OF BEANS, which suggests that you want the horse to be anything other than calm, so it may belong to the 'if in doubt, say it's to do with horse-racing' school of explanation (see, to name but a very few, A DARK HORSE, DOWN TO THE WIRE and BY A LONG SHOT). The French expression *prendre la chèvre*, 'to take the goat', confuses the issue further, as it means to be touchy, to be quick to take offence – ignoring the fact that goats are supposed to be soothing.

To be in someone's good books

This means to be in favour with someone, to have their good opinion, as opposed to being in their *bad* or *black books*. The *black* version is the oldest, dating back to the sixteenth century, when a black book was used to record financial transactions, domestic accounts and the like and, more sinisterly, the names of people 'liable to censure or punishment', as the *OED* puts it. The expression soon became metaphorical, so you could be in disgrace without your name necessarily being written down anywhere. Grose's *Dictionary of the Vulgar Tongue* (1785) has 'He is down in the black book, i.e. has a stain in his character.'

Once the literal *black book* had disappeared, there was scope for the phrase to develop; the variations *to be in someone's good* or *bad books* were both in use by the mid-nineteenth century.

Goody Two-Shoes

Goody Two-Shoes has had a bad press: she started off (in an anonymous story dated 1765) as a virtuous orphan called Margery Meanwell (the name says it all) who was so poor that she possessed only one shoe. When a kind gentleman gave her a pair of shoes she was so excited that she ran around pointing out to everyone she met that she had two shoes, and thus earned her nickname. The rest of the story shows her working hard and eventually being rewarded by marrying a rich man. They liked that sort of drivel (sorry, I mean 'improving tale') in the eighteenth century and Goody Two-Shoes was phenomenally popular.

The idea of calling a smugly virtuous person a *goody-goody* came along in the late nineteenth century (and in 1922 found its way into James Joyce's *Ulysses*), but it wasn't until the 1930s that *goody two-shoes* took on the same meaning. This is a bit hard on the original character: 'goody' in 1765 was short for 'goodwife' and was simply a respectful way of speaking to someone not grand enough to be called 'milady'.

Margery's tale is not the first use of the name Goody Two-Shoes: it appears a century earlier in Charles Cotton's *Voyage to Ireland in Burlesque* (1670) as a slang form of address to a bad-tempered woman:

> *Mistress mayoress complained that the pottage was cold;*
> *'And all long of your fiddle-faddle,' quoth she.*
> *'Why, then, Goody Two-shoes, what if it be?*
> *Hold you, if you can, your tittle-tattle,' quoth he.*

This suggests that the expression was in common use – perhaps at a time when poor folk were lucky to own any shoes at all – but there is no further record of it until Margery comes along.

It's (all) Greek to me

Shakespeare again: this time *Julius Caesar* (1599), Act I scene ii. The conspirators are worried that Caesar will be offered the crown of Rome – the Romans got rid of their tyrannical kings centuries ago and don't want them back, thank you very much. One of them, Casca, is reporting to his comrades what has been said in town earlier in the day.

'Did Cicero say anything?' asks Cassius.

'Ay, he spoke Greek.'

'To what effect?'

No idea, says Casca: 'Those that understood him smiled at one another and shook their heads; but, for mine own part, it was Greek to me.'

By speaking in Greek rather than Latin Cicero was showing off how educated he was, but today someone can be speaking to us in our native tongue and it can still go way over our heads if, say, they are talking about the latest IT developments or the DNA double helix. In Casca's case the words were literally in Greek; in the modern sense, they might as well be.

In fact, as often happened, Shakespeare popularized rather than invented this expression. At about the same time, Thomas Dekker used it in his play *Patient Grissill* in a jokey way that makes it clear his audience would have been familiar with it.

It may have come into English via the monks who transcribed classical manuscripts: at a time when even these scholarly personages may not have known Greek, they often wrote 'It's Greek, so it can't be read' alongside difficult passages. Only they wrote it in Latin, which is itself Greek to many.

Note that neither the monks nor Shakespeare used the word 'all'; nor do any of the *OED*'s examples. That seems to have snuck in – probably just for emphasis – some time in the twentieth century. For more about the English dismissiveness of things foreign, see TO GO DUTCH.

A gut feeling

This is neither more nor less than 'a feeling one has in the gut', something visceral, deep-rooted but probably not logical. Business guru Robert Heller (1932–2012) gave the sound advice, 'Never ignore a gut feeling, but never believe that it's enough.'

The expression seems to have existed only since about the 1970s, and in its earliest days was often used by scientists or economists by way of apology for putting forward an opinion that wasn't backed up by research or statistics. Which is, of course, what the rest of us do most of the time.

H

Hammer and tongs

This is very often preceded by *to go at it* and means to do something – a physical activity, a fight, a sexual act – vigorously and enthusiastically. The image comes from a blacksmith's forge, where the smith (generally 'a mighty man with large and sinewy hands', as Longfellow's nineteenth-century poem puts it) would use tongs to take his heated hammer from the fire and then bash away at the horseshoes or iron gate that needed to be knocked into shape.

The idiomatic use has been around in the UK since the early eighteenth century, when *hammer and pincers* is also found. The blacksmith would have used pincers to grip something firmly while he hammered it and *to go at something hammer and pincers* was used metaphorically of a horse that 'over-reached' itself, striking the hind foot against the forefoot.

The modern expression had moved firmly out of the forge and into the bedroom by the time Deborah Moggach came to write *Heartbreak Hotel* (2013). In that novel a woman who has never wanted children reflects that, at her age, 'any danger of that was long since past, even if she and Teddy were at it hammer and tongs, which was most certainly not the case.'

Hands down

To win *hands down* means to win easily, decisively, and the origin of the expression is simple. When a jockey sees that he is certain to win the race, he no longer needs to keep his hands tight on the reins by the horse's neck, nor raise his whip hand to urge the horse along. Have a look on YouTube to see the doomed Shergar romping home in the 1981 Derby and you'll see what I mean. The expression is older than that, though: it's first recorded in a racing context in 1867 and in a broader sense, referring to a man surrendering 'hands down, to a lot of trumpery complaints and grievances', in 1913.

As happy as Larry

This expression – meaning simply 'very happy' – has been common since the late nineteenth century, but no one seems to know who the original Larry was. The first recorded use is dated about 1875, from a New Zealand writer called G. L. Meredith, and may have referred to a hugely successful Australian boxer called Larry Foley. Alternatively, it may derive from the antipodean word 'larrikin', meaning a hooligan or one who is prone to larking about. Neither of them entirely satisfactory explanations, but as near as we can get.

We can't be much more definite about *as happy as a sandboy,* a British English equivalent. A sandboy (who was sometimes 'jolly' rather than 'happy') may have been a boy who sold sand – perhaps to somebody like Mr Boffin in Dickens's *Our Mutual Friend* (1864–5), whose fortune came from sifting through sand and seeing what valuables were hidden therein. Or he may have been a younger version of the sandman who throws dust in your eyes to make you go to sleep. Either way, why he should have been renowned for his jollity is unclear, though there is a suggestion from the nineteenth century that sandboys drank. This produces a 'which came first' conundrum that is neatly summarized by Dickens in *The Old Curiosity Shop* (1841): he describes a small roadside inn called the Jolly Sandboys, 'with a sign, representing three Sandboys increasing their jollity'.

To go haywire

Hay wire – it isn't rocket science, this one – is wire used to tie up bales of hay. You wouldn't recommend it for repairing sophisticated machinery. Thus in the USA in the early twentieth century there emerged the expression *a haywire outfit*, meaning one, particularly a logging concern, that made bodged repairs and ran things on the cheap. This may be the origin of the more widely used adjective *haywire* – erratic, out

of control or simply gone wrong. Alternatively that may come from the image of a long length of slim wire that has been wound up inefficiently and ends up in a chaotic mess. A combination of the two is the most likely explanation.

To go haywire, meaning to go awry or, of a person, to go distracted, is found in the USA in the 1920s and had crossed the Atlantic by the end of the 1930s. It's interesting that the first non-Americans to adopt American slang were often crime writers: the *OED* quotes both the British Margery Allingham and the New Zealander Ngaio Marsh – neither of them writing exactly 'hard-boiled' American-style thrillers – using this expression by 1940.

Head over heels

The original meaning of this expression was a literal one: *head over heels* meant upside down, topsy-turvy, the sort of position you're in when turning a somersault. More logically it should be *heels over head*, and indeed it used to be: the current phrasing is first found in the eighteenth century, whereas *heels over head* was used almost 400 years earlier, in a poem called *Patience*, by the author of *Sir Gawain and the Green Knight* (an unknown fourteenth-century poet whom scholars call, for their own convenience and for obvious if unimaginative reasons, the Gawain Poet).

Nowadays *head over heels* is almost always followed by *in love*. This expression seems to have been coined by, of all people, the American frontiersman Davy Crockett in 1834; later *head over heels* on its own was understood to mean 'in love' and John Galsworthy in *A Modern Comedy* (1924–8, the sequel to *The Forsyte Saga*) has a character refer to two young people as being simply *head over*.

Heads up

Normally found as *to give someone the heads up*, meaning to alert them to something that is likely to happen or to fill them in on something they have missed, this originated as a military command – if you bark 'Heads up!' in a sergeant-majorly sort of way, you expect your hearers to lift their heads. By the mid-nineteenth century it had moved out of the martial context to become a general expression of encouragement: as one citation in the *OED* has it, 'Heads up, you guys! … We ain't licked yet.'

Thus, particularly in the USA, *heads-up* came to mean 'competent, in the know' and, in the 1970s, 'in the form of an advance warning', as in *a heads-up alert* of action that was about to be taken. The transfer from adjective to noun and to the current expression took place in the 1980s, when business jargon was, as they say, hitting the ground running and actioning its deliverables.

To bring to heel

To force someone or something to be obedient, as when you make a dog walk beside you in a disciplined fashion. The figurative sense dates from the second half of the nineteenth century when, for example, the scientist T. H. Huxley referred to passions being 'trained to come to heel'.

Hell for leather

This odd expression means 'very fast', with a hint of desperation or recklessness. Kipling makes the sense of urgency clear when, in *The Story of the Gadsbys* (1891), he has one character instruct another, 'Here, Gaddy, take the note to Bingle and ride hell-for-leather.' No one seems quite sure why, but one probable explanation is that the rider would

137

be kicking his horse on to ever greater speed and to hell with the effect on his own boots or the horse's saddle and stirrup leathers.

There is an American expression *hell-bent for leather*, which dates from about the same time and means much the same thing, though it can also convey zealousness or determination. It has been suggested that this comes from an arduous walk that was damaging to shoe leather. So whether the expressions emerged with the British Army in India or in the American Wild West, the result is the same: you're going to wear out your shoes.

High and dry

With AS BOLD AS BRASS and BATS IN THE BELFRY we had alliteration; here we have a rhyme that helps to make an expression catch on. At its simplest if you are high up on the shore and dry because you are away from the water, you are stranded – particularly if you are a fish or a boat. The expression is first recorded in a London *Times* shipping report of 1796 and describes a vessel that has gone aground and is literally *high and dry*.

The idiomatic sense of being OUT ON A LIMB, without support, was in use by the end of the

nineteenth century: in 1881 the politician Sir Edward Hamilton wrote in his diary, 'Meanwhile, Dr. Flood's successor had been appointed, and Dr. Flood was left high and dry without preferment.'

A 1954 film called *High and Dry* concerns a wealthy American who is conned into using an elderly and unseaworthy boat to transfer his valuable possessions to a remote Scottish island. Entirely at the mercy of the conniving skipper Mactaggart, the American risks finding that everything he possesses is, well, low and wet, to be pedantic about it, but that wouldn't have been nearly such a catchy title.

No holds barred

'No ring • No ref • No rules' boasts the poster advertising the 1989 film *No Holds Barred,* starring the wrestler Hulk Hogan, and that is approximately what this expression means, both in and out of the wrestling fraternity. In the early days of wrestling – and today in spin-offs such as cage fighting – there were very few rules and certainly no holds were forbidden. The modern Olympics feature both Graeco-Roman and freestyle wrestling, one of the differences between them being that in the Graeco-Roman form holds below the waist *are* barred.

As with most idioms, the expression has, over time, developed a wider application. It can now be used to refer to anything from politics to pornography (though come to think of it in the latter context it may also have a literal application).

(To eat) humble pie

Umbles – a common foodstuff in the fourteenth century and recently rescued from obscurity by Heston Blumenthal – are the entrails or offal (the heart, liver, etc.) of an animal, usually a deer. They would commonly have been eaten 'below stairs', quite possibly made into a pie, while the nobility in the Great Hall ate the more glamorous cuts of meat. The diarist Samuel Pepys, who was neither a servant nor a noble but had a hearty appetite, records in 1662 having been given a present of some venison, 'so I had a shoulder roasted, another baked, and the umbles baked in a pie'.

There is a phenomenon in linguistics called metanalysis, which means changing the form of a word to make a new word, and particularly changing the point where words are divided. If that is as clear as mud, think of 'an apron', which derives from the Old French word *naperon* and would once have been 'a napron'. Why am I telling you this? Because 'umbles' were originally 'numbles' and the form of the word changed over time. A second

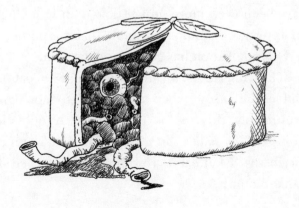

phenomenon, known as hypercorrection, means putting right something that wasn't wrong in the first place. Many people habitually drop the *h* at the start of a word, so the uneducated trying to appear educated often put it back whether it belongs there or not. Thus is it not uncommon to hear people talking about 'happles' or 'Hamerica', and thus 'umbles' became confused with 'humble'. The fact that an umble pie was commonly eaten by humble people made the new form sound all the more probable.

The metaphorical sense of *to eat humble pie* – meaning to apologize grovellingly – is found in the nineteenth century. An early user, the novelist Charles Reade, went one further and had his character eat 'wormwood pudding and humble pie'. Wormwood being notoriously bitter in taste and what the *OED* calls 'grievous to the soul', this would have been even more indigestible than humble pie on its own: we should be grateful that this particular verbal humiliation has gone out of fashion.

The Americans, by the way, tend to eat not umbles but crow when they need to apologize: presumably this too is unpleasant. A quotation from the *San Francisco Picayune* dated 1851 puts it succinctly: 'I kin eat a crow, but I'll be darned if I hanker after it.'

K

To kick the bucket

The best guess is that this odd metaphor for 'to die' relies on an unfamiliar meaning of the word 'bucket'. Nothing to do with the thing you take to the seaside, this is a yoke or beam on which something could be hung or carried. An entry in the *New English Dictionary* of 1888 tells us that 'the beam on which a pig is suspended after he has been slaughtered is called in Norfolk, even in the present day, a "bucket". Since he is suspended by his heels, the phrase to "kick the bucket" came to signify to die.'

The first part of this is certainly true: animals were once slaughtered in this way and it is likely that any creature in its death throes would kick out at anything within reach. Whether this is the origin of the expression remains open to question.

It is also suggested (in an article by Thomas de Quincey dated 1823) that a would-be suicide stood on a bucket in order to arrange the rope that would hang him, then kicked it away; and that the victim of a lynch mob was similarly left dangling once a bucket was removed. However, the idiom is older than either of these sources would indicate, which tends to make the pig-slaughtering story the best of a not entirely satisfactory bunch.

L

A last-ditch effort

This is a final, desperate effort – if it fails, all is lost. The metaphor comes from the battlefield, where the last ditch would be the last part of your defences as you retreated. Prince William of Orange is quoted as saying in 1672, 'There is one way to avoid [witnessing the destruction of my country]: to die defending it in the last ditch.' Considering he was at war with France, England and two separate German states at the time, it's a remark bordering on the foolhardy, but he lived to tell the tale: he became King William III of England, the male half of 'William and Mary', and didn't die until 1702. Some 150 years after William's bold remark, Thomas Jefferson wrote about 'a government driven to the last ditch by the universal call for liberty' – moving away from warfare but still referring to conflict.

More recently, *a last-ditch effort* can be made in many walks of life, as this quote from communications guru Marshall McLuhan (1911–80) shows: 'Good taste is the first refuge of the non-creative. It is the last-ditch stand of the artist.' And, in case you think that sounds like just a smart-alec line from someone obsessed with the media, you should know that McLuhan is also quoted as saying, 'I don't necessarily agree with everything I say.'

To learn the ropes

To learn how to do something, particularly in the sense of following appropriate procedures; doing whatever it is the way a certain organization likes it to be done. The origin is likely to be nautical, applied to a novice sailor learning how to manipulate the ropes that controlled the sails. Less probably, it may be theatrical and refer to the ropes used to raise and lower scenery. The expression appears in both those contexts in the USA in the nineteenth century, but soon broadened: by 1948 Evelyn Waugh was writing in *The Loved One*, 'Dennis was spending his last week at the Happier Hunting Ground in showing him the ropes.' If you've read the novel you'll know that the Happier Hunting Ground is a pet cemetery and will understand that there, too, strict procedures have to be followed, to avoid upsetting the grieving but wealthy clients.

To leave in the lurch

Perhaps surprisingly, 'lurch' here is not connected with staggering about; instead it comes from an old French game, *lourche*, which was known in the seventeenth century and was probably something like backgammon. Just as in backgammon a player can be gammoned – beaten by an embarrassing margin – so in *lourche* a player could be *in the lurch*. The expression was used in a number of other games, including cribbage and whist, to indicate that the losing player had scored fewer than a specified number of points. From this *a lurch* came to mean any awkward position and by the end of the sixteenth century someone who was *left in the lurch* had been abandoned by friends and supporters and was forced to cope alone with unexpected difficulties.

To do one's level best

Change 'level' into 'very' or 'absolute' here and you have the meaning. One of the earliest recorded uses (1873) is as the title of a short story by the American writer Edward Everett Hale, about a young man who is advised on his wedding day that 'now you have a position in society you must assist in all good objects.' The groom promises to do 'his level best' and his sincere endeavours land him in the poorhouse.

No one is quite sure why 'level' came to have this meaning, but at about the same time as Hale was writing his story, *on the level*, meaning honourable, sincere, also appeared; perhaps there is an overlap between the good intentions of the two expressions. See also FAIR AND SQUARE.

To go out on a limb

This seems to have come into being as a fully fledged idiom: there's no record of its being used to describe someone literally climbing a tree, crawling along a branch and having it cut out from beneath them. It means, if you'll excuse the mixed metaphor, to stick your neck out at the risk of having the rug pulled from under your feet – to find yourself without support in a difficult position. It emerged in the USA at the end of the nineteenth century.

One of Shirley MacLaine's volumes of autobiography is entitled *Out on a Limb* and the actress has been quoted as saying, 'Don't be afraid to go out on a limb. It's where all the fruit is.' Maybe so, but the traditional meaning of the idiom advises against it.

In the limelight

In the nineteenth century, limelight – an intense white light obtained by heating lime – was much used in theatres to highlight important actors and scenes. A performer who was *in the limelight* was therefore the centre of attention. By the start of the twentieth century you didn't have to be in the theatre to be *in the limelight*; the term could apply, as it does now, to anyone in the public eye.

In 1952, Charlie Chaplin called his last American film *Limelight*; it's a sentimental and much ridiculed story about a fading music-hall comedian who is inspired by a young ballerina to achieve a final hour of triumph. Although by now Chaplin is talking (rather too much, the critics said, as if he were making up for all those years of not being able to), *Limelight* is interspersed with the 'intertitles' common in the silent era: one announces, 'The glamour of limelight, from which age must pass as youth enters.' Take a Kleenex or be prepared for a good laugh, depending on your mood.

To be at loggerheads

To be in dispute, to have a bitter and probably long-standing row with someone. In Shakespeare's time a loggerhead was the equivalent of a blockhead – someone who wasn't very bright, the implication being that their head was made of wood. A logger was a particular kind of block, one that was fastened to a horse's leg to keep it from running away. Loggerhead turtles, loggerhead shrikes and loggerhead kingbirds are all so named because they have comparatively large, flat-topped heads.

But none of this seems to have much to do with falling out with someone. The likely explanation for the expression is that 'loggerhead' had a literal meaning that pre-dates the Shakespearian figurative one: it was an iron instrument with a long handle, used for heating liquids and melting pitch. The iron head would have been heated to a high temperature in the local forge, so a loggerhead would have been a powerful weapon for an angry blacksmith to swing at someone who annoyed him. See also HAMMER AND TONGS.

Long in the tooth

As we age our gums tend to recede, making our teeth look longer; this is true of people but even more so of horses, whose teeth continue to grow throughout their lives. Looking in a horse's mouth, therefore, could tell a prospective buyer whether or not the animal had much working life left in it. (*Looking a gift horse in the mouth*, of course, was considered impolite, but it was a different matter if you were parting with cash.)

Oddly, since the experts tend to agree that the expression derives from horses, the first recorded use describes a person, a character in William Makepeace Thackeray's *Henry Esmond* (1852) who was 'lean, and yellow, and long in the tooth; all the red and white in all the toyshops of London could not make a beauty of her'. This poor woman's cousin, Thomas Esmond (our hero's father), has returned from military service abroad with no money and is looking to make a wealthy marriage: he thinks of her as 'a woman who might be easy of conquest, but whom only a very bold man would think of conquering'.

Thackeray, it should be said, had a jaundiced view of marriage: in the early chapters of his masterpiece *Vanity Fair* he says, 'This I set down as a positive truth. A woman with fair opportunities and without a positive hump, may marry whom she likes.' Imagine the furore if he posted *that* on Twitter.

By a long shot

'By a long way, by far' – often used in the negative: 'That wasn't the whole story – not by a long shot.' This is 'shot' in the sense of *to have a shot*, meaning

151

to have a try, or *a shot in the dark*, a random guess or attempt. Although it sounds as if it ought to be connected with shooting, *by a long shot* seems to have originated in the American horse-racing world, where *a long shot* means a horse backed at long odds. The figurative sense is first found in the 1840s.

The similar *by a long chalk* dates from about the same time and refers to the habit in some games of marking out distances or keeping the score with a piece of chalk.

M

Middle of the road

In the 1970s a band called Middle of the Road recorded one of the most irritating songs ever to reach the Number 1 spot, 'Chirpy Chirpy Cheep Cheep'. The very fact that it was so irritating (once you got it into your head you were humming it all day, despite the fact that you hated it) made a nonsense of the group's name, because in a musical context *middle of the road* is tuneful but unadventurous, unlikely to offend anyone. That's what it means in a broader sense, too: avoiding extremes, moderate, never happier than when you can find a fence to sit on.

Many commentators have observed that *middle of the road* is a misnomer for a safe, even bland, position, because it is surely safer to choose a side of the road and stick to it: preferably the left in the UK and the right in most of the rest of the world. Or, if you are a pedestrian, to avoid the road altogether. In fact, *middle of the road* should really have been *middle of the political spectrum*, because it was born out of (American) politicians not wanting to alienate voters. The expression is first recorded in the late nineteenth century, but in 1927 the journal *American Speech* summed it up neatly: 'The "middle of the road" is the sacred path followed by compromising politicians who desire to promote their own or their party's fortunes.' In 1996 the *New York Review of Books* put into words what many people had been thinking all along: 'Those who occupy the middle of the road in politics risk getting run down from both directions.'

A moot point

One that is subject to debate or argument, unable to be firmly resolved. For hundreds of years in Anglo-

Saxon England a moot was a meeting of a local council, where matters of interest to the community were discussed. A question raised at a moot was therefore to be discussed and arbitrated upon and 'to moot' has meant to discuss or dispute in a court of law for well over a thousand years. The first recorded use of *moot point* is in 1563, when Doctor Laurence Humphrey, President of Magdalen College, Oxford, published a book called *Nobles or of Nobilitye*, designed to instruct the nobility in how to educate their sons. He advised 'that they be not forced to sue the lawe, wrapped with so infinite crickes and moot poyntes'.

Nowadays, people who aren't old enough to remember what a moot was – and, like policemen, historians do seem to be getting younger and younger – have been known to refer to this concept as *a mute point*. Perhaps they feel that it is something we ought to keep quiet about; in any case, it is another example of folk etymology (see TO CURRY FAVOUR).

To keep mum

From as early as the fourteenth century, 'mum' has meant an inarticulate sound through closed lips – 'mmmm', in effect. *To keep mum*, therefore, is simply to keep quiet. *Mum's the word*, to drag in another related expression, has been around since the sixteenth century, as has *to play mum*. The idea of *keeping mum* appeared in the nineteenth.

None of this, of course, has anything to do with 'mum' meaning 'mother' – or it didn't until the Second World War, when posters disseminating the warning that 'careless talk costs lives' were a feature of government propaganda. 'Be like Dad, keep Mum' was one punning catchphrase. Another poster in the same campaign showed a glamorous woman surrounded by men in uniform, all too obviously smitten with her charms. 'Keep mum, she's not so dumb' was the slogan. No more capital *M*, you notice – this is a far from maternal type. Men were urged to be discreet in the presence of women like this, who were, by implication, almost certainly enemy agents. Well, there was a war on.

N

Neck and neck

This expression emerged from horse-racing as far back as the seventeenth century: two horses evenly matched, surging towards the finishing line, the neck of one almost indistinguishable from the neck of the other. It's a vivid piece of imagery, because horses have long necks (unless, I suppose, you are comparing them with giraffes) and they do seem to stretch out as an eager racer nears the winning post.

People have been metaphorically *neck and neck* since the beginning of the nineteenth century, when the *Morning Post*, reporting on a local election, remarked that 'The contest for Kent is the keenest that has yet been run. The three candidates are *neck and neck*. You might cover them all with a sheet.'

It's a pity that 'so close you might cover them all with a sheet' hasn't stood the test of time: that's a vivid piece of imagery, too.

Neck of the woods

'A narrow stretch of land, usually with water on either side' is quite a familiar meaning for 'neck'; more specifically, and originally in the USA, it once also meant 'a narrow stretch of wood, pasture, ice, etc'. So *neck of the woods* is arguably a tautology, but also arguably just a way of specifying exactly what sort of neck you are talking about. In the days before street addresses – indeed, in the days before streets in colonial America – a *neck of the woods* was a small settlement on a given piece of land. Nowadays *this neck of the woods* tends to mean little more than 'around here, near where I live'.

To get it in the neck

'Catch' or 'take' may be substituted for 'get' in this expression, but whichever way you phrase it it means to be hit hard by something, or to be strongly reprimanded. It appeared in the USA at the end of the nineteenth century, but was familiar enough in Britain for H. G. Wells to use it in *The War in the Air* in 1908. The origin is straightforward enough: if someone hit you in the neck with a bullet, say, or even an overripe tomato, you would feel it strongly. The same applies to an unpleasant reproof.

To nip something in the bud

If you literally nip a plant in the bud, you stop it from flowering; if what you figuratively nip is an idea or an activity, you stop it from going any further. Early uses – from the sixteenth and seventeenth centuries – seem to have been concerned with preventing the development of inappropriate love affairs. But by 1746 the clergyman James Hervey, in his *Meditations among the Tombs*, was making the poignant observation that the King of Terrors (death) seemed to have inverted the laws of nature: 'Passing over the Couch of decrepit Age, he has nipped Infancy in its Bud; blasted Youth in its Bloom; and torn up Manhood in its full Maturity.' In other words, the tombstones showed many people who had died before their time.

More recently and more frivolously, American comedian Dennis Swanberg used the expression as the punchline of a sketch in which a Southern preacher repeatedly and rhetorically asks his congregation, 'What shall we do with sin?' A little boy in the back pew, trying to be helpful, suggests, 'You've got to nip it in the bud.' Out of the mouths of babes and sucklings, some might say.

The nitty gritty

This is normally something that you *get down to* and it means to stop BEATING AROUND THE BUSH and start considering the important or practical aspects of a situation. The expression arose in the USA in the mid-twentieth century, but no one really knows why: it has been suggested that 'nitty' refers to nits or head lice, or that 'gritty' means the grit left at the bottom of a barrel, though there is no hard evidence in either case. Whatever the truth may be, the additional, rhyming word was probably added to produce a slick-sounding phrase.

The website of the long-lived American country-folk-rock group The Nitty Gritty Dirt Band admits that they began by hanging out in a guitar shop in Long Beach, California, trying to 'figure out how not to have to work for a living'. A perfectly reasonable ambition, but it doesn't give any real insights into where the name came from.

O

Off one's own bat

Cricket seems first to have been played in England towards the end of the sixteenth century and had become widespread by the end of the seventeenth. The most common way of scoring is *off one's own bat* – i.e. by hitting the ball and running between the wickets. (If American readers choose to read 'bases' rather than 'wickets' in that last sentence, they will see that the concept is not entirely alien to them.) There are other ways of making runs, but cricket fans will know them already and non-fans won't care, so let's leave it there.

Early uses of *off one's own bat* all refer specifically to cricket; the first figurative use – meaning

independently, using one's own initiative – didn't appear until 1845, when the Reverend Sydney Smith wrote of a fellow clergyman that he 'had no revenues but what he got off his own bat'. (He must have been hard up, poor man – clergymen were not well paid and it was only by having a private income that they were able to live in those elegant rectories you still see scattered about England.)

It's always fun to have an excuse to mention Sydney Smith, as he was one of the great wits of his day; here is a singularly appropriate *bon mot* of his: 'Poverty is no disgrace to a man, but it is confoundedly inconvenient.'

Off the beaten track

This is fairly self-evident: if you go *off the beaten track* you stray into the undergrowth or uncharted territory. The eighteenth-century poet Edward Young was one of the first to give the idea of a *beaten track* being a rut. He wrote a meditation on life and death called *The Complaint* (or *Night-Thoughts*) in which he decided that living forever, and therefore never getting to heaven, would be dreadful; it included the lines:

> *to climb life's worn, heavy wheel,*
> *Which draws up nothing new? to beat, and beat*
> *The beaten track?*

Since then, and since the invention of independent, 'adventure' travel, getting *off the beaten track* has come to be seen as a good thing and is part of many an advertising slogan for companies with names such as Undiscovered Destinations. Though as one world-weary response to an online article on the subject pointed out, 'Now that you've told us all about them, we can look forward to these places being on the beaten track pretty soon.' See also ON A SHOESTRING.

Off the cuff

To do something *off the cuff* is to do it spontaneously, without preparation – although the origin of the expression suggests that you did in fact prepare and that you used notes written on your cuff as an *aide-mémoire*. Some of today's sources say that the first people to use their cuffs in this way were Hollywood directors: they would make notes during one 'take' so they didn't forget what they wanted to say to the actors before the next. Others suggest that writing notes on a cuff was an aid to after-dinner speakers. Either way, the concept arose in the USA in the early twentieth century and had taken hold by 1938. That is the date of this endearing quote from the *New York Panorama*, a series of essays produced by the Federal Writers' Project: it is defining 'a humorously conceived system of language corruption' called *double talk*:

> *Double talk is created by mixing plausible-sounding gibberish into ordinary conversation, the speaker keeping a straight face or dead pan and enumerating casually or off the cuff.*

P

To paint the town red

The website of the Melton Mowbray Town Estate – a charitable organization established in 1549 for the benefit of the local community – regales us with the story of the Marquis of Waterford, who attended the local races with some friends one night in 1837 and, returning in an inebriated condition, refused to pay the toll that permitted him to enter the town. When the gatekeeper tried to insist on his due, the Mad Marquis, as he was affectionately known, barricaded the man into his house and proceeded to paint the tollgates red. He and his friends are said then to have gone on the rampage and painted much of the rest of the town red, too.

This may or may not be true, though the Marquis's reputation for revelry is well documented. Counting somewhat against it for the purposes of this book is the fact that the expression *to paint the town red*, meaning to go out and indulge in riotous behaviour, first appeared in *The New York Times* almost fifty years later, in 1883. No one is sure where it came from. 'To paint' is old (British) slang for 'to drink', because drinking causes the face to turn red, but this is probably irrelevant to the American usage. Some sources suggest a connection with the blood spilled when drinking turns to violence; others have linked the idiom to the red-light areas traditionally inhabited by prostitutes – but there is no concrete evidence for any of this. Personally, I think Melton Mowbray has taken *painting the town red* so thoroughly to its bosom that we should let it hang on to it. There's no saying what shade your face might turn if you ate too many of its pies.

Beyond the pale

This is generally thought of as 'pale' in the sense of a pointed piece of wood used to make a fence, and thus the fence itself and the area enclosed by it. Historically there were several significant 'pales', perhaps the most famous being in Ireland – it was the part of the country under English jurisdiction, which varied over the centuries according to who had won which skirmish lately. In nineteenth-century Russia, the Pale of Settlement was the area in which Jews were obliged to reside. People described as *beyond the pale* may, therefore, have been English who mingled (horror of horrors) with the Irish, or

Jews who strayed where the authorities said they had no right to be.

The *OED*, however, tells us that there is no early evidence for these theories and that they are more likely to be later rationalizations of a phrase that hasn't been adequately explained. As early as the fifteenth century, 'pale' had the figurative meaning of a limit or safeguard; to cross it was to go beyond accepted bounds or to transgress. That is the modern meaning of the expression: to break the rules of acceptable behaviour, to the extent of making oneself a social outcast. In *The Pickwick Papers* (1837), Dickens relates an argument between the rival editors of two small-town newspapers, which ends with Mr Pott darting Mr Slurk 'a look of contempt, which might have withered an anchor', and saying to him, 'I consider you, sir, a viper … I look upon you, sir, as a man who has placed himself beyond the pale of society, by his most audacious, disgraceful, and abominable public conduct.' If you read that in a suitably blustering, spluttering, outraged tone, you'll know all you need to know.

To palm something/someone off

'He promised me a diamond ring, then palmed me off with a cheap imitation'; 'He palmed the cheap imitation off as a diamond ring' – either way, deception has been perpetrated. Mark Twain (1835–1910) had a more imaginative take on this: 'Nothing seems to please a fly so much as to be taken for a currant, and if it can be baked in a cake and palmed off on the unwary, it dies happy.' But the expression is appreciably older than this: Tobias Smollett, translating Cervantes' *Don Quixote* in the mid-eighteenth century, has the tantalizing 'My lord duke has palmed his lacquey upon us, in lieu of my lawful husband.'

The best guess at the origin of all this is that it is associated with hiding something in the palm of the hand, either to steal it or to cheat at cards.

To pan out

In suggestions such as 'Let's wait and see how it pans out', this is a neutral expression – it could go either way, good or bad. But it can also be used as 'I'm sure it will all pan out', meaning it will pan out well, be all right in the end. The expression originates in the California Gold Rush of the 1840s and '50s, when 'panning' for gold meant shaking a sample of earth through a pan or sieve to get rid of the debris and leave only the gold. If you were lucky, that is. The American explorer Paul Leland Haworth later gave it a specific twist in his book *Trailmakers of the North West* (1921): 'The Colonel had told them that a cubic foot of gravel would pan out twenty dollars in gold.' Without having read the book or knowing much about Gold Rushes, I can't help feeling a lot of the speculators would have discovered that the Colonel was overly optimistic.

Part and parcel (of)

Way back in the days of Chaucer's *Canterbury Tales* (around 1395), one of the meanings of 'parcel' was 'an integral part': in 'The Franklin's Tale' there is mention of something being *parcel of someone's woe*. From this developed the tripping-neatly-off-the-tongue phrase *part and parcel*, used in a legal context to mean the same as 'parcel' on its own – one piece of property was deemed, for the purposes of defining ownership, as *part and parcel* of another larger one.

This precise meaning lasted all the way from the fifteenth to the nineteenth centuries, when the concept finally widened to refer to almost anything that was an integral part of anything else. German Chancellor Angela Merkel combined it with another similar idiom when she said, 'I said, yet again, for Germany, Europe is not only indispensable, it is part and parcel of our identity. We've always said German unity, European unity and integration, that's two parts of one and the same coin.' If she said it in German, she probably said *einen wesentlichen Bestandteil*, which translates literally as 'an essential constituent part', suggesting that Germans don't use the expression often enough to feel the need for an idiom.

Not a patch on

Meaning 'nothing like as good as', this is another slightly mysterious saying: it may originally have been 'no more than a patch on', meaning a small and inferior way of repairing something of better quality. If that is true, the version we use today – and have been using since at least 1860 – is more or less nonsensical, but so be it.

In a pickle

A pickle was originally a hot sauce served with meat, which evolved into the vinegary concoction full of chopped up bits and pieces that we use today. (This is in British English, as opposed to the American pickle, which Brits call a gherkin.) Whether it was used to liven up bland fare, to help preserve it or to disguise the fact that it was beginning to go off, when you put something into a pickle, it isn't going to come out again in a hurry or in the same condition. Thus to be *in a pickle* is to be in a mess – *in a stew*, to use another idiom with the same implication – from which you are not going to extract yourself easily. It can also mean just untidiness: a character in Henry Fielding's *Joseph Andrews* (1742) rather breathlessly expresses embarrassment in front of an unexpected visitor: 'She was ashamed to be seen in such a pickle, and that her house was in such a litter; but that if she had expected such an honour from her ladyship she should have found her in a better manner.'

The metaphor has been around since at least the sixteenth century; Shakespeare in *The Tempest* (1610) is an early user, when he has the King of Naples address the jester Trinculo, who is clearly drunk: 'Where should they find this grand liquor that hath gilded them? How cam'st thou in this pickle?' It's tempting to suggest that Shakespeare is punning on the use of 'pickled' for 'drunk', but that sense isn't found until the nineteenth century. He just means that his character has got himself into something of a state.

Pie in the sky

Thinking of the sky as heaven will help with the meaning here: it is the promise of unlikely good things to come at some unspecified future date. The expression derives from a 1911 song called 'The Preacher and the Slave', written by Joe Hill, leader of an early American trade union called International Workers of the World. The song parodied a style of hymn that was very popular at the time: the underprivileged were promised joy, leisure and all the food they could eat in the next life in return for the misery and starvation to which they were doomed in this one. 'Work and pray, live on hay, you'll get pie in the sky when you die,' wrote Joe. In your dreams, he muttered under his breath.

Nowadays we might describe an idea or a business plan as being *pie in the sky*, but the implication is the same: don't mortgage your house on the strength of it.

A piece of cake

The American poet Ogden Nash wrote in 1936 that life was *a piece of cake*, meaning much the same as the singer and actress Ethel Merman had meant a few years earlier when she maintained that life was *just a bowl of cherries*. The expression then seems to have joined the (Second World) War Effort and been adopted as RAF slang for an easy task or mission – or perhaps a difficult one that the boys were determined to be brave about. Certainly that nuance was sufficiently entrenched in the public mind for the British novelist Derek Robinson to call a 1983 work about an RAF fighter squadron *Piece of Cake*. The book was adapted into a TV mini-series a few years later and, forty years after the war, no one seems to have felt that the title needed to be clarified for a modern audience.

From pillar to post

Meaning 'from one place to another and probably back again, without achieving anything', this expression was originally *from post to pillar* and seems to have referred to the way a ball was knocked around a real tennis court: the net was tied to a post at one side of the court and to a pillar supporting the stands at the other. Positioning the ball so that your opponent had to run back and forth across the court was a favourite ploy of the superior player. (Imagine a similar tactic in an oversized squash court and you'll have the general idea.)

Real tennis became popular in England at the time of Henry VIII (1509–47) and the expression is first recorded shortly after his death. A quotation from 1602 confirms the origin, and also suggests that 'post' could be pronounced to rhyme with 'cost' rather than 'host': 'Euery minute tost, Like to a tennis ball, from piller to post.' The usefulness of this rhyme may help to explain why the original word order was changed; after all, there can be only so many times that you need a rhyme for 'miller' or 'Aston Villa'.

Spanish has an equivalent expression, *to go from Herod to Pilate*, recalling how Christ was shuttled *from pillar to post* before being condemned to be crucified; the Dutch say *to be sent from cupboard to wall* (and presumably smash your face into the latter), while the French have *to jump from a cock to a donkey*, a graphic description of an act of complete futility.

With a pinch of salt

Adding *a pinch of salt* to food is done to make it more flavoursome, more palatable, so it's slightly odd that the idiom should refer to something that one doesn't believe. It's even odder that the first more or less modern use should be in a biblical commentary. But so it is. There is a particularly dramatic verse in the Book of Revelation in which it is said that this is a time of persecution and that the faithful will have to wait until some more of them are martyred before they can have any hope of salvation. In 1647, an English theologian called John Trapp remarked of the verse that *this is to be taken with a grain of salt*. He presumably meant that the grain of salt would make this unpalatable news more acceptable, but back then it was surely rather shocking to suggest that the Bible was not to be taken literally.

Over the centuries, the expression has been toned down somewhat. Instead of making something unpleasant more acceptable, it has become a way of suggesting that we shouldn't take someone too seriously. A boaster, a know-all, a newspaper columnist who is paid to be controversial – these are all people whose views may be taken *with a pinch of salt*.

To pipe down

This is a slightly politer but still colloquial way of saying 'to shut up': it can also be used in the imperative as a firm request, probably to a boisterous child, to cool it a little. It dates from the early nineteenth century and its origins are nautical, *to pipe down* meaning to signal (by playing on a pipe) to sailors that it is time to retire for the night.

Amid the cacophony of the modern world many of us may have sympathy with the aims of Pipedown, the campaign against piped music, which its website describes as 'one of the under-recognized scourges of contemporary life'. You have to shudder to imagine what the founders of this organization, who find the gentle strains of elevator music an intrusion on their private space, would have thought of someone playing the hornpipe to tell them to go to bed.

In the pipeline

A comparatively recent idiom, spawned by the oil industry in the mid-twentieth century. Something that is *in the pipeline* is literally on the way from supplier to customer or metaphorically in the process of development, nearing completion. It's used in business or in politics – new measures may be *in the pipeline* for the next session of Parliament – but also by musicians and film stars talking about future projects. Actor Hugh Dancy is quoted as saying (with applaudable common sense), 'As always, there's a couple of things in the pipeline, but that pipeline is a strange and ambiguous place.'

To go to pot

Nowadays this means *to go to rack and ruin*, to fall apart through neglect or (of a person) to be ruined. In the seventeenth century, it was more drastic: 'Poor Thorp, Lord Chief Justice, went to Pot, in plain English, he was Hang'd,' wrote Edmund Hickeringill in 1682.

The origins of the idiom are even earlier: originally *to go to* the *pot*, meaning to be chopped into small pieces to go into a stew, it was used in a metaphorical sense by, among others, the medieval scholar Erasmus. He wrote in his *Apothegmes*, translated into English in 1564, of Herod's order that all the little children be killed 'and how among them Herod's own son had gone to the pot'. Herod gets a bad press, but it seems unlikely that even he intended his child to be diced up and served in a casserole – put to death, maybe, but not necessarily in that gruesome way.

Nowadays the meaning is less terminal: in the 1970s an Australian transport magazine, describing a certain vehicle's brakes, observed – with a cavalier disregard for mixed metaphors – that 'it can throw a spanner in the works if the adjustment setting goes to pot'.

See TO GO HAYWIRE for another idiom born of messes with machinery.

To pull out all the stops

If you *pull out all the stops* on an organ, you crank the volume up as far as it will go. To do this metaphorically means to make a great effort – either to achieve something (meeting a deadline, perhaps) or to put on a great display (for a twenty-first birthday party). For an example of the idiom used in a non-musical sense, it's hard to beat one of the first to be recorded, in Matthew Arnold's *Essays in Criticism* (1865): he referred to the unpopular task one was undertaking 'when one tries to pull out a few more stops in that powerful but at present somewhat narrow-toned organ, the modern Englishman'. A century and a half later, that rustling sound you hear is an awful lot of women nodding sagely as they read those words.

To pull someone's leg

Opinions vary on this one – did you *pull someone's leg* when he was hanging from the gallows, as a friendly gesture to hasten his demise and put him out of his misery? If so, it is a bit of a stretch (no pun intended) to get from there to the modern colloquial meaning of 'to tease or deceive someone in a good-humoured way'. Or did you pull a leg out from under someone, either to make him easier to rob or to make him fall over and look ridiculous? If so, 'pull' is an odd verb to choose – you'd have thought 'knock' might be more appropriate.

Whatever the origins, the expression *to draw someone's leg* was in use in Scotland in the 1860s and *to pull ...* is found in the USA in the 1880s, both without inverted commas, explanation or apology, indicating that they were familiar phrases that had already been around for a while.

To pull the wool over someone's eyes

This is a more serious form of deception than *pulling someone's leg* (see previous entry): the latter is a joke, whereas *pulling the wool over someone's eyes* could involve dishonesty or swindling. It derives from the time when gentlemen wore powdered wigs over their hair; if you jerked the fleecy-looking accessory over their eyes, they couldn't see where they were going and could be either literally robbed or metaphorically blinded or bamboozled.

The expression's first recorded use is from the USA in 1839, although the wearing of wigs

had long since gone out of fashion there, and all the *OED*'s nineteenth-century citations are from North America. The (terribly British) author P. G. Wodehouse used it in the 1930s, but he had by that time had stints in Hollywood and his younger characters often used the sort of racy slang they might have picked up at the cinema. *To pull the wool over someone's eyes* wouldn't fit into that category nowadays, but it would have been enough to raise a formidable aunt's eyebrows back then.

To push the boat out

To help someone push a stranded boat out into the water so that he can get on his way is an act of generosity; so too is *pushing the boat out* in terms of buying expensive presents or providing lavish hospitality. The expression can also be used more loosely to describe any act of mild extravagance.

It found its way into naval slang in the 1920s, despite the fact that most of the boats the navy owns would take quite a bit of pushing; and it appeared in a non-naval context about the same time. Today in northeastern Scotland there is a literary publication called *Pushing Out the Boat*, which welcomes submissions in English, Doric or Scots. I don't know about you, but for me submitting in Doric would very much be pushing the boat out.

To pussyfoot around

Derived, obviously, from the way a cat walks, this means to move stealthily, or to act in a cautious, equivocal way, avoiding unpleasantness, confrontation or any form of decision-making. 'Pussyfoot' was originally an adjective (an American usage from 1899 describes an outspoken politician who didn't believe in 'trying to win by pussy-foot methods'), but the concept of *pussyfooling around* appeared only a few years later, again in the context of politics.

In America during the Prohibition period, a pussyfoot was also a teetotaller, an advocate of Prohibition or, more generally, a killjoy. A man called William E. Johnson (1862–1945), a leader of the wonderfully named Anti-Saloon League, was nicknamed 'Pussyfoot' because of his advocacy of sobriety; and there was even a Pussyfoot Cocktail made from the disgusting-sounding combination of orange juice, lemon juice, grenadine and egg white. You don't often hear a stronger argument in favour of tequila slammers.

R

To take a rain check

If it rains hard enough during a baseball match, play is abandoned, or at least postponed, and disappointed ticket-holders are given *a rain check* so that they can get in for nothing next time. (This is the same American use of 'check' that gives them the concept of a hat-check girl – you give her your hat when you go into a restaurant or theatre and she gives you a check, or ticket, so that you get your own property back when you are ready to go home.) Detachable stubs on tickets were invented by Abner Powell (1860–1953), baseball player turned manager and club owner, who also introduced the concepts of Ladies' Day, to keep the fair sex away from unsavoury types in the crowd, and of covering the ground with a tarpaulin so that play could resume quickly after rain. Another of those people who ought to be famous but you've probably never heard of.

Anyway, *to take a rain check* came to mean to refuse an invitation but with the clear intention of accepting another time. The literal concept has been around since the 1880s; the metaphorical one is nicely summed up in this *memento mori* quote from the *Daily Kennebec Journal* of Augusta, Maine, in 1903: 'If you expect to do anything to make people remember you, it is time to get at it. St Peter isn't going to issue any rain checks.' It's not far removed from the Latin *carpe diem*, but perhaps not many people in Augusta, Maine, were reading Horace in 1903.

As so often with American-born expressions, this one crossed the Atlantic courtesy of a thriller writer. In 1976, in Len Deighton's *Twinkle, Twinkle, Little Spy*, we come across the surprising: '"Let me take a rain-check." "On a love affair?" I said.'

Raining cats and dogs

It may be that in the bad old days before decent sewage, cats and dogs caught in violent rainstorms were drowned and washed through city streets along open drains. Or they may have been washed down from their hiding places in thatched roofs.

Alternatively, given that other idioms for heavy rain invoke stair rods or, in the French equivalent, a spear-like medieval weapon known as a halberd, it may just be that heavy rain gave the impression of heavy things falling out of the sky. The concept is an international one: the website omniglot.com gives variations in over forty languages. Frogs feature more than once, as does the idea that the rain is being poured from a bucket or tub. Of the remainder, perhaps the most appealing are the Welsh *It's raining old ladies and sticks*, the Czech *It's raining wheelbarrows*, the Norwegian *It's raining female trolls* and the Danish *It's raining shoemakers' apprentices*.

The English expression is several hundred years old: in the mid-seventeenth century one writer referred to *raining dogs and polecats* and another to *dogs and cats*, but the modern wording seems to have taken grip by 1738, when Jonathan Swift used it in *Polite Conversation*. The *OED* references come under the entry for 'cat and dog', which it defines as 'referring to the proverbial enmity between the two animals … Full of strife; inharmonious; quarrelsome'. So it may be that at times of heavy rain the animals don't just fall heavily from the sky; they brawl and squabble as they do so.

To rest on one's laurels

The laurel tree was sacred to the Greek god Apollo, who is often depicted with a laurel wreath round his head; so too are Roman emperors and triumphant generals, the wreath being a sign of honour. (The word 'laureate' – to describe a winner of a Nobel Prize or a poet who composes verse for royal weddings – comes from this concept.) *To repose on one's laurels*, therefore, came to mean to retire from battle or from public office, but to do so with dignity, conscious of a job well done. The modern pejorative sense of relying on previous glories and not bothering to try to achieve anything further elbowed its way in during the nineteenth century: Percy Bysshe Shelley (1792–1822) wrote that 'Nothing wilts faster than laurels that have been rested upon' and a century later the philosopher Ludwig Wittgenstein (1889–1951) was giving it the full modern meaning: 'Resting on your laurels is as dangerous as resting when you are walking in the snow. You doze off and die in your sleep.'

To give one's right arm for something

Assuming you are right-handed, giving your right arm is a huge sacrifice. Actually, come to think of it, it's quite a sacrifice if you are left-handed. It means you really, really want something. Sharpe's *London Journal of Entertainment and Instruction* (1849), a periodical with the high moral tone typical of the Victorian era, gives an early example of the expression: in a short story included therein, a young governess has returned to the bosom of her family (as they would doubtless have said in those days) for her first holiday in two years; in the course of an emotional reunion, her twelve-year-old brother 'looked at Lizzy as if his heart would break; and he felt as if he could gladly give his right arm to be cut off if it would make him, at once, old enough to go and earn money instead of Lizzy.'

Less drastic but out of the same stable is *to give one's eye teeth for something*: the eye teeth, so called because they sit directly under the eyes, are what we now call the upper canines. The name has been around since the sixteenth century, but the first recorded use of the expression dates only from 1930.

See also TO COST AN ARM AND A LEG.

As right as rain

It means absolutely fine, hunky dory, tickety-boo – but, apart from the alliterative appeal, why should it have come into being? Unless you are a farmer in a drought-ridden country, what's right about rain?

Over the centuries, we have at various times said *as right as a ram's horn*, *as right as a line*, *as right as ninepence* and *as right as a trivet*. Well, a line is by definition straight, a trivet stands firmly on its three feet and 'ninepence' became proverbial in the seventeenth century in the form *as fine as fippence, as neat as ninepence*. Presumably this last version just sounded right and people subsequently said *as grand as ninepence* or *as right as ninepence* without caring that it was meaningless. More problematic is a ram's horn, which is noticeably curly: perhaps the original sense was that it was solid and reliable.

But rain? Disappointingly, there really seems to be no better explanation than the alliterative one. It's been in use for well over a hundred years, and even though Adele has written a song asking 'Who wants to be right as rain?' and what she says carries a lot of weight among the young, it seems unlikely to go away any time soon.

To ring the changes

A wonderfully British expression, because it derives from that wonderfully British activity, bell-ringing. A 'change' is the different order in which a peal of bells can be rung, and there are lots of them. Linda and Roger Flavell, in their *Dictionary of Idioms*, have saved me the trouble of doing the sums: they note that 'in a bell tower boasting twelve bells it would be possible to ring a total of 479,001,600 changes, which would take some thirty-eight years.'

In idiomatic use, *to ring the changes* means to do things in different ways, often just for the sake of it, introducing change for change's sake. This sense dates back to the seventeenth century and has, to all intents and purposes, been used – ha! – unchanged ever since.

Between a rock and a hard place

This is normally prefaced by *caught* and now means to be faced with a choice between any two unpleasant alternatives. When it was first used – in the USA in the 1920s – it seems to have referred specifically to mining workers in Arizona. A banking crisis some years earlier had caused problems for the mining companies, who refused their workers' demands for better pay and conditions. The miners were therefore faced with the choice of putting up with the uncomfortable status quo or seeking employment elsewhere. Journalists writing about their plight came up with this expression.

An older and more scholarly place where you don't want to be caught is *between Scylla and Charybdis,* the rock shoal and whirlpool that posed a danger to sailors in the Straits of Messina, between Sicily and mainland Italy. *Between the devil and the deep blue sea* is the maritime equivalent of being *caught on the horns of a dilemma*, and the fact that we have so many ways of expressing the concept suggests that we find ourselves in this unfortunate position quite a lot.

To rub someone up the wrong way

Try rubbing your cat's fur the wrong way and see how she likes it. That's the origin of the expression, which dates from the 1830s and in the idiomatic sense simply means 'to irritate'.

Run of the mill

Mills – whether they produce flour, clothes or lumber – are geared up to do the same thing over and over again and churn whatever it is out in quantity, without perhaps paying much attention to quality control. To do something different, more bespoke, requires adjusting the settings, introducing other raw materials and grinding, stitching or cutting in a different way. Anything manufactured in this way is likely to be more expensive than the day-to-day stuff, the *run of the mill*. The idiom, which seems to have originated in North American lumber mills, has been in use since the 1870s.

S

To get the sack

There was a time when a skilled worker would own his own tools and take them away with him – in a sack – if he was dismissed from a job. This is commonly held to be the origin of the expression, though I must say it seems unlikely to me. A skilled worker's tools would have been his most valuable possessions – surely he would have carried them back and forth every day rather than leaving them on, say, a building site? However, the same image has been known in French since the seventeenth century (although it is now obsolete) and in Dutch since before that. It didn't appear in English until the early nineteenth century, so perhaps we simply adopted a handy expression without thinking too much about it. *To give someone the sack* dates from about the same time.

John Camden Hotten's *Slang Dictionary* of 1867 mentions *to get the sack* in the same breath as *to get the bullet* – 'the connexion of which with discharge is obvious', as he expresses it, rather pompously. Moving from pomposity to condescension, he puts both phrases in a paragraph about what he somewhat patronizingly calls 'operatives' or workmen's Slang', which is, 'in quality but slightly removed from tradesmen's Slang'. I'm glad to have had the opportunity of clearing up any little doubts you may have had on that subject.

Up to scratch

This was originally *up to* the *scratch* and probably comes from boxing, in the days when boxers used to take their positions at the start of a bout by putting their toes against a scratched mark.

A more idiomatic sense has, however, been around for some time: in the 1840s both Dickens and Anne Brontë used *come* or *bring up to the scratch* about people, meaning that they needed the courage or honour to do what was required of them; in 1911 George Bernard Shaw used it in *Getting Married*, with reference to getting a bridegroom to turn up on time on his wedding day. The idea of something inanimate *not being up to scratch* (and it is very often now used in the negative), meaning 'not of the required standard', emerged as recently as the 1970s.

To have a screw loose

The origin of this expression is not hard to deduce: something that *has a screw loose* is likely to fall apart, fall off the wall or otherwise come to grief. At first – from the early nineteenth century – it meant that something was awry or dishonest: using the first of these senses, Dickens in *Martin Chuzzlewit* (1844) has the amiable Mark Tapley offering himself as an unpaid servant and travelling companion to the eponymous hero, remark, 'I see well enough there's a screw loose in your affairs.' A generation later, in *The Eustace Diamonds* (1873), Anthony Trollope has an impecunious peer pondering whether or not to propose to a rich but dishonest woman:

> *To have his wife, immediately on her marriage, or even before it, arraigned for perjury, would not be pleasant … But a man does not expect to get four thousand pounds a year for nothing. Lord George, at any rate, did not conceive himself to be in a position to do so. Had there not been something crooked about Lizzie – a screw loose, as people say – she would never have been within his reach.*

He clearly doesn't mean that Lizzie is insane, but that there is something socially unacceptable, slightly suspect about her. It wasn't long, however, before the expression had come to be synonymous with being eccentric or mentally disturbed. In 1928, in the irreverent literary magazine *The American Mercury*, Carl Sandburg made it clear to the most inattentive reader: 'There was a screw loose somewhere in him, he had a kink and he was a Crank, he was nuts and belonged in a booby hatch.' I think we get the point.

All at sea

The *OED*'s definition of the figurative sense of *at sea* is hard to improve on: 'in a state of mind resembling the condition of a ship which is out of sight of land and has lost her bearings'. Just in case you aren't familiar with that somewhat specific state of mind, it has this helpful addition: 'in a state of uncertainty or perplexity, at a loss'. *At sea*, in this idiomatic sense, has been around in the UK since the eighteenth century; the *all* was added, presumably for emphasis, in the late nineteenth.

To sell someone down the river

This expression, meaning to betray someone who trusts you for some underhand reason of your own, originates in the slave-owning states of the USA. By the early nineteenth century it was illegal to import slaves, so there arose a substantial internal trade. Selling someone 'down the river' meant sending them down the Mississippi to the slave markets of New Orleans or Natches, whence they might be sold to goodness knows where, but almost certainly away from home and family. On the lower reaches of the Mississippi conditions were also said to be harsher than they were further north, so being *sold down the river* was deemed a suitable punishment for a badly behaved slave. The literal nature of the expression is shown in this example from 1836:

> *Suppose it be enacted that after the year 1840 slavery shall cease to exist in Kentucky. What would follow? All who chose would sell their slaves down the river; the benevolent would free them, and send them away, or let them remain, as they thought best.*

Nowadays it is likely to be employees rather than slaves who have been badly treated, but the concept is the same. Nor does the selling have to be done to someone else: as early as 1927 P. G. Wodehouse wrote in *The Small Bachelor*:

> *When Sigsbee Waddington married for the second time, he to all intents and purposes sold himself down the river. To call him a cipher in the home would be to give too glowing a picture of his importance.*

To shake a stick at

Nineteenth-century American English had the disparaging expressions *not worth shaking a stick at* or *nothing to shake a stick at*. Shaking your stick was a gesture of defiance, so something you couldn't be bothered shaking it at was beneath contempt.

However, the modern expression refers not to a lack of quality but to an abundance of quantity: *more than you can shake a stick at* means 'a lot'. No one is quite sure where this change of meaning comes from: using a stick to count livestock? Maybe. Counting fallen enemies on the battlefield? Hmm. The new idiom seems first to have been recorded in Lancaster, Pennsylvania, in 1818, when the local journal announced that 'We have in Lancaster as many Taverns as you can shake a stick at' –

presumably in order to encourage tourists to come along and PAINT THE TOWN RED.

Three sheets to the wind

A sheet in nautical parlance is, perhaps surprisingly, not a sail but a rope or line that fixes the sail in place. (If you were ever in the Guides or Scouts you may have learnt a knot called a sheet bend, for joining two ropes of different sizes.) If the ropes were not tied properly, the sail would lurch about drunkenly, hence the idiomatic expression – originally *in the wind*, now almost always *to the wind* – meaning to be extremely drunk. It dates from the early nineteenth century, when it could be adapted to describe various degrees of drunkenness: Catherine Ward in *The Fisher's Daughter* (1824) writes that the long-suffering 'Wolf replenished his glass at the request of Mr. Blust, who, instead of being one sheet in the wind, was likely to get to three before he took his departure.' See also TO LEAVE IN THE LURCH.

On a shoestring

The string or thong used to tie a shoe is proverbially thin and of little value: 'I will accept nothing belonging to you, not even a thread or the strap of a sandal,' says Abram to the King of Sodom in the biblical book of Genesis. So to do something *on a shoestring* means to do it cheaply, with a very limited budget. Early uses – in the USA at the end of the nineteenth century – often refer to petty gamblers operating *on a shoestring*; by the 1920s this had shifted to start-up businesses that had no wealthy venture capitalists behind them; and the modern idiom also embraces the budget traveller. An online travel company called shoestring.com offers, for example, 'India and Nepal on a shoestring'; its shout line is the appropriately punning 'Go further'.

Short shrift

'To shrive', in the Roman Catholic Church, is to hear the confession of a penitent and to impose a penance ('Say ten Hail Marys'), so that the penitent's sins are forgiven – or 'shriven'.[2] The act of confessing and receiving absolution is therefore a 'shrift'. A criminal (or political opponent) who had been condemned to death was permitted to confess and to cleanse his

---

[2] It's also where we get Shrove Tuesday from, which may be a sobering thought next time you are tossing a pancake.

soul before being executed, but was often forced to be quick about it – hence, *to make short shrift*.

The first recorded use is in Shakespeare's *Richard III* (1594), when Richard, still Duke of Gloucester, has sentenced Lord Hastings to death and refuses to eat until the execution has been carried out. One of Richard's underlings addresses the condemned man with the tactless words:

> *Dispatch, my lord; the duke would be at dinner:*
> *Make a short shrift; he longs to see your head.*

This literal use persisted for some centuries before the expression turned figurative in the nineteenth. In modern parlance, we tend not to *make* short shrift so much as to *give* it to someone, meaning to treat them with impatience and a lack of sympathy or not to give credit where credit is due. When the film *Argo* came out, for example, in 2012, former US President Jimmy Carter observed that it concentrated on the achievements of the American CIA, glossing over the Canadian role in resolving the Iranian hostage crisis that lies at the heart of the film. A headline in *Macleans* announced that Carter believed the film 'gave short shrift to Canada' – though *Macleans*, being a Canadian magazine, may have felt it had AN AXE TO GRIND.

As sick as a parrot

In the 1970s it seemed as if every football manager, player or fan who suffered a disappointment was *as sick as a parrot* about it. It wasn't anything to do with nausea; it was more like, to use another vaguely physiological idiom, feeling *gutted*. Specifically, it was the opposite of the obligatory *over the moon*, used by those whose team had won.

Why a parrot? Sadly there seems to be no connection to the fabled *Monty Python* 'Dead Parrot' sketch of 1969; it's more likely that a few widely reported cases of psittacosis (parrot fever – a disease common among caged birds that has

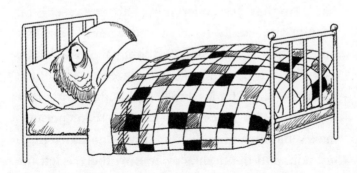

some very unpleasant symptoms when it is passed on to humans) caught the public imagination. Why it should have come so quickly to be associated almost exclusively with football is one of those little mysteries with which the study of language abounds. Perhaps it is because footballers were, on balance, no more articulate then than they are now and using the same simile as everyone else simply saved thinking.

By the skin of one's teeth

A Biblical misquotation from the book of Job. Job (pronounced Jobe) is, you may remember, the man who is beset by all sorts of troubles in order to test his faith in God. Eventually, his three 'Job's comforters' having proved no use at all, he is bemoaning his fate. He has lost everything he possessed, his friends and family have turned against him: 'My bone cleaveth to my skin and to my flesh, and I am escaped with the skin of my teeth.' This is the text from the King James Bible (1611), but an earlier translation, by Miles Coverdale in 1535, perhaps makes the meaning clearer: 'My bone hangeth to my skin, and the flesh is away, only there is left me the skin about my teeth.'

What it boils down to is that poor Job, who has done nothing to deserve all this, has wasted away and has lost everything except the skin of his teeth. Not quite what we mean today, when – to use another metaphor pertaining to the jaw – we have *a close shave*. The original meaning of having lost everything one owned persisted until the eighteenth century. Then in the early nineteenth we find: 'Having escaped "by the skin of my teeth", I may be allowed to look back upon the dangers I have passed and with the voice of salutary warning point them out to others.' These are the words of a Methodist missionary called Joshua Marsden, describing the pitfalls into which younger preachers may fall if they set out, as he had done, to convert the heathen of Nova Scotia and New Brunswick. Joshua's use of inverted commas shows that the expression is novel and perhaps even a bit risqué for a man of his calling, but it soon caught on.

To smell a rat

Here's a great opportunity to mix a metaphor, because *to smell a rat* means to think something is fishy; that is, to suspect dishonesty or deception. The expression has been around since the sixteenth century and it is likely to have come from a combination of the unpleasant smell of a dead rat and the fear of rats as carriers of disease.

Spick and span

Either 'brand new and still shiny with newness' or 'so thoroughly cleaned that it looks like new'. Both the words are old: 'span' comes from an Icelandic word for a chip of wood, so 'span-new' (used by Chaucer in the fourteenth century) meant 'as new as a chip off the old block'; 'spick' is related to 'spike' and 'splinter'. The two words had been put together to make a pleasing phrase by the seventeenth century.

Dr Samuel Johnson, who didn't always get things right, suggested (in his 1755 *Dictionary*) that 'span' came from an Old English word for 'to stretch'; 'span-new' was 'therefore originally used of cloth that was extended or dressed at the clothiers, and *spick-and-span* is newly extended on the *spikes* or tenters'. Modern authorities now disagree, but I quote him because of the connection with tenters mentioned under ON TENTERHOOKS. Johnson also describes *spick and span* as 'a low word', one 'I should not have expected to have found authorised by a polite writer'.

Sorry, Sam, it's perfectly OK now.

A stamping ground

This was originally – in the USA – applied to animals such as bison which stamp the ground to mark their territory or to warn off intruders. Thus their *stamping ground* was the core of their territory, the place where they were most often to be found and the one they would defend most fiercely. When the expression came to be applied to people (in the 1820s) it took the same meaning and could refer to one's home town, favourite bar or neighbourhood shopping centre, to name but three.

To steal someone's thunder

A sad story, this one. An English playwright named John Dennis (1657–1734 and no, I'd never heard of him either) came up with the idea of rattling a sheet of tin to create the effect of thunder in a play of his. Called *Appius and Virginia*, it was neither a critical nor a popular success but the 'thunder sheet' proved to have its uses. Shortly after *Appius and Virginia* had closed – prematurely, in its author's view – Dennis was in the audience in the same theatre for a production of *Macbeth*. There is, in the Scottish play, a fair amount of bad weather, particularly any time the witches appear. Hearing the sound effects, Dennis cried out something along the lines of 'Damn them! They will not let my play run, and yet they steal my thunder!'

The idiomatic use of *to steal someone's thunder*, meaning to win praise for something that should be credited to someone else, is not recorded until 1900, almost two centuries later, but that may be because the story had appeared in a book of literary curiosities published in 1893 and given poor Mr Dennis (if not his play) a new lease of life.

A stick in the mud

A pole or stick in any substantial depth of mud is likely to be, well, stuck – and the idiomatic use describes a person in that position: unable to move because their feet are bogged down, usually because they lack the imagination or initiative to move them. From the nineteenth century it has been used as a noun ('He's such an old stick-in-the-mud') or as an adjective ('He was none of your humdrum, stick-in-the-mud, old-fashioned practitioners'), often contemptuously but also with just a soupçon of affection. And, like so much of the English language, it has tended to lose its hyphens as time has passed by.

No strings attached

It's tempting to wonder if this idiom has anything to do with puppets: a person (or puppet) who has *no strings attached* is free to act as they like. But I can find no evidence of this and, come to think of it, a puppet with no strings attached would just fall down in a crumpled mess of arms and legs.

No, the explanation seems to be that one definition of 'string' is a cord or lead used for controlling an animal. If a horse, say, has *no strings attached*, it is free to roam at will. If a business deal, romantic relationship or other arrangement has *no strings attached*, the parties to it are also free to do what they like.

Although variations appeared – in the USA – in the late nineteenth century, one of the earliest users of this exact form of words was communications expert Marshall McLuhan, who appeared under A LAST-DITCH EFFORT; he referred (in his first book, *The Mechanical Bride*, published in 1951) to the rather more abstract concept of 'imagination with no strings attached'. In less visionary mode, the expression is also often used with reference to loans, particularly political ones, or to aid impoverished countries. In both these contexts, it always comes as a surprise if money is paid out *without* strings being attached. There is, after all, *no such thing as a free lunch*.

A swansong

For at least 2,000 years there has been a widely held but erroneous belief that swans, having failed to sing all their lives, produce a particularly poignant call when on the point of death. Pliny the Elder, the great natural historian of the first century AD, observed that this wasn't true, but the idea has hung in there – both Chaucer and Shakespeare refer to it. The first recorded use of the idiom is by the Scottish minister John Willison in the eighteenth century: in a collection of *Scripture Songs* he quotes the last words of the dying David (from the second Old Testament book of Samuel) as the king's Swan Song in the face of death. A metaphorical *swansong*, *swan song* or *swan-song* (though the hyphen, like the swan, seems to be at death's door) is therefore a farewell appearance by an actor, musician, politician or sports star – anyone, in fact, who has been in the public eye and is now bowing out. See also IN THE LIMELIGHT.

T

To a T

There is much debate about this expression, confused by the suggestions that *T* may be short for 'tee' or for 'tea'. More likely is that it is short for 'tittle', a small stroke or point in writing or printing which makes small but important distinctions between one character and another. It's been around since Latin was widely written, but in modern use it is applied, for example, to the French cedilla (ç) and the Spanish tilde (ñ), both of which alter the pronunciation of the letter to which they are attached.

From this meaning, 'tittle' came to be a very small and accurate part of anything and *to a tittle* to indicate great precision. Which is what *to a T* now means: 'it fits you to a T' is another way of saying 'it fits you exactly.' In this abbreviated form the idiom has been around since the seventeenth century.

To talk the hind legs off a donkey

This really is to talk. To talk and talk without letting up. There is a school of thought that says the expression originates in Ireland (proverbial home of the garrulous and persuasive, see THE GIFT OF THE GAB) and takes account of the fact that donkeys and horses do not normally sit down on their behinds the way, say, dogs do. *To talk the hind legs off a donkey* (and in early uses sometimes *a horse*) is therefore to talk so wearisomely that the animal collapses under the sheer weight of words.

Nice, and possibly true. The idiom is found from the early years of the nineteenth century.

On tenterhooks

A tenterhook is – or was, in the heyday of the weaving industry – a hook used to attach a piece of woven cloth to a tenter, a wooden frame which prevented the cloth from shrinking or losing its shape. Tenters were once commonly placed in rows outside mills or factories in areas known as tenting grounds or tenting fields. However, given that most such places were in parts of the North of England notorious for their heavy rainfall – naming no names but Manchester knows where it is – it was eventually deemed prudent to bring them indoors.

To be *on tenterhooks* was therefore to be strung up, under tension, and the idiomatic meaning of the expression is just that: to be in a state of nervous anticipation, waiting for something – possibly unpleasant – to happen. Although the concept had been around for several hundred years before the eighteenth century, the first recorded use of the expression comes in Tobias Smollett's novel *Roderick Random* (1748): 'I ... left him upon the tenter-hooks of impatient uncertainty.'

That's the ticket

It could be the winning ticket in a lottery, or the ticket on which candidates' names were put forward for election (from which derives the sense of 'ticket' meaning the policies on which a candidate or party is running). Whatever the origin, the expression has been around since about the 1830s, originally in the USA, and now means 'That's the right thing; that's just what we need.'

To toe the line

The first thing to point out here is the spelling: it is not *to tow the line*. To put your toe up to the line is to be in the correct position for starting a race; thus *to toe the line* (or occasionally *to toe the mark*) means to follow the rules, to submit to authority, particularly unwillingly. It is first found in the early nineteenth century and by the end of the century had found its way into politics, where an individual refusing to *toe the party line* remains an issue that rears its head every now and again.

Every Tom, Dick and Harry

Some say (read that in a mysterious, spooky-story-by-the-fireside sort of voice, if you would) that this expression is connected with the devil, because both Dick and Harry are alternative names for him (see WHAT THE DICKENS?) However, that theory hits a stumbling block when you come to Tom. There is no evidence that this name was ever used in this way; instead it was for centuries a generic word for a man of the people. In any case, why would an expression meaning 'anyone, a group of the average men in

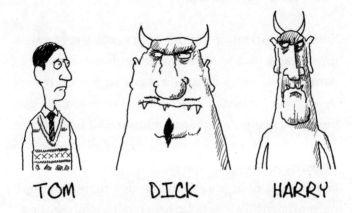

TOM   DICK   HARRY

the street' have reference to the devil? It would be asking for trouble.

Much more likely is that the three simply came together as being common names and, in their abbreviated forms, the names of ordinary folk. *The Vocal Miscellany: a collection of above 400 celebrated songs,* dated 1734, gives the flavour with 'Farewell, Tom, Dick, and Harry, Farewell, Moll, Nell, and Sue.' Not Thomas, Richard and Henry, nor Mary, Eleanor and Susan, which are the names the toffs would have been known by.

Tongue in cheek

Some interpretations of this expression suggest that if you speak with your tongue literally in your cheek, your face contorts in such a way that it is clear you don't mean to be taken seriously. I'm not sure: I've been practising in front of a mirror and find it very difficult to say anything intelligible at all.

Early examples, however, suggest that putting one's tongue in one's cheek signified contempt rather than the more light-hearted 'I'm only teasing' sense it has today. Webster's Online Dictionary gives a very specific origin: 'Spanish minstrels would perform for various dukes in the 18th century; these dukes would silently chastise the silliness of the minstrel's performances by placing their tongue firmly to the side of their cheek.' And the *OED*'s earliest citation – from that rich source, Tobias Smollett's *Roderick Random* (1748) – also indicates that it is the gesture rather than any spoken accompaniment that matters. In much the same way you might shrug your shoulders, raise an eloquent eyebrow or, if you are well versed in Shakespearean abuse, bite your thumb.

By the mid-nineteenth century, however, people had moved the literal tongue back into its normal position. They were now able to speak metaphorically *with their tongue in their cheek*, saying something insincere, sarcastic or, as time wore on and memories of the phrase's origins faded, simply flippant.

A turn up for the books

'He said, "I'm going to chop off the bottom of one of your trouser legs and put it in a library.' I thought, "That's a turn-up for the books."'

That's an old Tommy Cooper joke and you probably have to remember that great comedian (who died in 1984) to think it's funny.

Never mind.

A turn up, in this context, is in any case nothing to do with trousers; it's a pleasant surprise and has been since at least the middle of the nineteenth century. 'The book' – the expression originally used the singular – was the kind that bookmakers used, so *a turn up for the books* was what happened when an unfavoured horse won and the bookies didn't have to pay out much. Although in common use on the racecourse, the phrase doesn't seem to have ventured into the wider world until the 1950s.

W

Wet behind the ears

If you're ever around a farm when a lamb or a calf is born, you'll see that it's wet not just behind the ears but all over: it comes out covered in what I believe in medical circles is called goo, which the mother licks off. She then licks her baby in all sorts of places to make it stand up, feed, understand basic bodily functions and so forth. No wonder it's wet.

Human mothers don't generally lick their offspring in the same way (not in public, anyway), but this is another example of an expression that started off in a specific and literal sense being adopted into a general metaphorical one. *To be wet behind the ears* originated as soldiers' slang at the time of the First World War and refers to someone who is naïve and innocent of the ways of the world, often in an annoying way. Telling someone they are wet behind the ears is frequently followed by the exasperated suggestion that they should grow up.

A wet blanket

Ever been camping after a wet day's walking and found that somebody has dumped his sodden cagoule on your sleeping bag? Not pleasant. That is the sort of feeling that a metaphorical *wet blanket* casts over the people he or she is with.

In fact, the expression evolves from a more useful application of a wet blanket – to put out a fire by smothering it. In 1772 the dramatist Richard Cumberland marked the transition from literal to figurative use in his play *The Fashionable Lover*: 'His humours damp all mirth and merriment, as a wet blanket does a fire', and Byron said much the same thing in *Don Juan* fifty years later: 'Lambro's reception at his people's banquet/Was such as fire accords to a wet blanket.' Not the most powerful rhyming couplet he ever wrote, perhaps, but one doesn't want to be *wet-blanketty* about it, nor to be accused of *wet-blanketiveness* (these are both variations from the 1830s and '40s, quoted in the *OED*, which sadly seem not to have caught on).

To give someone/something a wide berth

This is a nautical expression, a berth being in modern parlance either 'a place in a harbour for a ship' or 'a bunk in a ship', but in earlier times 'a place where there is room to moor a ship'. Sailors were warned to give something a *clear* or *good berth*, meaning to keep a safe distance from it. 'Berth' is found in this literal sense throughout the seventeenth and eighteenth centuries; it moves into idiom thanks – as so often – to Walter Scott who, in his *Letters on Demonology and Witchcraft* (1829, now available as a Kindle edition, if you're interested), wrote, 'Giving the apparent phantom what seamen call a wide berth.' This is also the first recorded instance of *giving a wide berth* to a person (or at least a phantom) rather than a thing.

In the course of the nineteenth century the expression gradually moved away from seafaring to its current, wide-ranging use. The English satirist Max Beerbohm (1872–1956) was never one to miss the opportunity for a *bon mot* (as a young man he moved in the same circles as Oscar Wilde, so had to live up to a certain standard). He had this advice for life in general: 'Anything that is worth doing has been done frequently. Things hitherto undone should be given, I suspect, a wide berth.'

The world's your oyster

Shakespeare's *Merry Wives of Windsor* (*c*.1600): 'Why then the world's mine Oyster, which I, with sword will open,' boasts Pistol, when Falstaff refuses to lend him money. What he means is that he will take his sword and attack anyone he pleases, using his sword to open their purses. What we mean nowadays is less ferocious and more likely to be legal: the world is full of opportunities and we are eager to make the most of them.

Catchy though it is, the expression seems to have lain dormant for 200 years after Shakespeare's time; then a translation of Alain-René LeSage's picaresque novel *Gil Blas* came up with 'invested with full powers to make the world his oyster, and leave nothing but the shell to his unpatented competitors'. Since then it has been in frequent and broad-ranging use, as any traveller on the London Underground will know.

The wrong end of the stick

The source of this expression is disputed, because it was originally *the short end of the stick*, which, commentators rightly remark, makes precious little sense. The most likely explanation is that 'short' was a euphemism for another word beginning with *sh* and ending with *t*. It's obvious enough why the sh*tty end of the stick should be the unpleasant one; the question is why it should have become sh*tty in the first place. Use your imagination, be as disgusting as you like and you won't be far wrong, seems to be the consensus. Perhaps this offended people, because *the wrong end of the stick* had come into use by the time John Heywood's *Workes: a dialogue containing proverbs and epigrams* was published in 1562. Then, and until about the 1930s, it meant to be at a disadvantage in a bargain, probably because someone had 'done the dirty' on you.

Over time the expression evolved to the modern meaning of getting the facts wrong, not understanding what is going on. Evelyn Waugh gave it a nice twist in *Vile Bodies* (1930):

My private schoolmaster used to say, 'If a thing's worth doing at all, it's worth doing well.' ... But these young people have got hold of another end of the stick, and for all we know it may be the right one. They say, 'If a thing's not worth doing well, it's not worth doing at all.'

A high moral note on which to end?

Bibliography

Rachel Best & Jean-Christophe Van Waes, *Excuse My French!* (Kyle Books, 2013)

Julia Cresswell, *The Cat's Pyjamas: the Penguin Book of Clichés* (Penguin, 2007)

Linda and Roger Flavell, *Dictionary of Idioms and their Origins* (Kyle Cathie, 1992)

——, *Dictionary of English Down the Ages* (Kyle Cathie, 2nd edition, 2005)

Caroline Taggart, *An Apple a Day* (Michael O'Mara Books, 2009)

——, *Pushing the Envelope* (Michael O'Mara Books, 2011)

Website references

The following sites provided much useful information:

IMDb, www.imdb.com
Oxford Dictionaries Pro, english.oxforddictionaries.
   com
OED Online, www.oed.com
The Phrase Finder, www.phrases.org.uk
Thinkexist.com
YouTube, www.youtube.com
Worldwide Words, www.worldwidewords.org

and the odd snippet came from:

www.azlyrics.com
www.biography.com
www.boston.com
www.brainyquote.com
www.dictionary.reference.com
www.english.stackexchange.com
www.funwithenglishblog.com
www.grammarphobia.com
www.idioms.yourdictionary.com

www.joe-ks.com

www.knowyourphrase.com

www.lyricsmania.com

www.lyricstime.com

www.medicalpastiche.blogspot.co.uk

www.meltonmowbraytownestate.co.uk

www.mumsnet.com

www.nationalarchives.gov.uk

www.neatorama.com

www.onestopenglish.com

www.parliament.uk/about/living-heritage

www.pbs.org

www.pinterest.com

www.pipedown.info

www.pushingouttheboat.co.uk

www.spartacus.schoolnet.co.uk

www.stampinggroundfestival.co.uk

www.thefreedictionary.com

www.therecordmine.com

Tinyonline, http://users.tinyonline.co.uk/
    gswithenbank/sayindex.htm

www.uk.answers.yahoo.com

www.victorianweb.org

Wikipedia, http://en.wikipedia.org

www.wordwizard.com

www.yachtsandyachting.com